Announcing the Word of God

ANNOUNCING
THE WORD OF GOD

by JOSEF A. JUNGMANN

Translated by RONALD WALLS

1967
HERDER AND HERDER NEW YORK
232 Madison Avenue, New York 10016

Original edition: *Glaubensverkündigung im Lichte der Frohbotschaft,* Innsbruck, Vienna, Munich, Tyrolia-Verlag, 1963.

Nihil obstat: John M. T. Barton, Censor Librorum
Imprimatur: ✠ Patrick J. Casey, Vicar General of Westminster
    August 8, 1967

Library of Congress Catalog Card Number: 68–17328
ⓒ 1968 by Burns & Oates Ltd.
Printed in the United States

Contents

Preface

It is essential for the Church constantly to adapt her work to changing circumstances. Just as the work of maintaining the fabric of a great building is never finished, so in the life of the Church sections are continually having to be replaced, damage repaired, improvements made. In our time such work has assumed a scope quite unknown to previous generations. A reorganization of pastoral work has begun, which seeks to bring about the regrouping of society and the expansion of all horizons. The growth of relevant literature in periodicals and books, and the emergence of new sciences like the sociology of religion, are but symptoms of this.

Most of these efforts are along the lines of organization, more intensive application or more correct use of present means and energies. Even such efforts as those of the Better World movement are no exception. But in all this, theological reflexion ought not to be neglected. This is what we have in mind when we speak of pastoral theology. And, indeed, such reflexion is at work at various points, not to speak of the industrious rebuilding around theology itself. In this book I have tried to sum it up critically, and, where possible, develop it. The book takes up the same theme as that of a book I published a quarter of a century ago, and which, because of the novelty of some of its arguments, received a very mixed reception.[1] Today the arguments contained in this book need no longer fear the charge of novelty; but they may suffice to clarify and

[1] *Die Frohbotschaft und unsere Glaubensverkündigung*, Regensburg, 1936.

advance many ideas that are already at work at different points.

This book, it is to be hoped, follows the same lines that the Second Vatican Council in its first session laid down for the renewal of the Church, and which are remarkably in harmony with the directive given by Pope John XXIII when he opened the council on 11 October 1962: the formulation of the deposit of faith 'depends, for its structure and harmony, upon the needs of the magisterium whose main function is that of the pastoral ministry'.[2]

Innsbruck,   JOSEF A. JUNGMANN, S.J.
February 1963

---

[2] *A.A.S.*, LIV, 1962, p. 792. Tr. in *Report from Rome*, London, 1963, p. 102.

I

The Situation

IT IS many years ago now since Father Hitz, the Redemptorist preacher, said that the modern world was made up of neo-pagans, neo-Christians, and habitual Christians.[1] Almost at the same time a well-known Viennese parish priest was making even gloomier affirmations. Out of every twenty Catholics he found only one who really practised his faith in an effective way. The number of those who practised was equalled by the number of those who definitely turned their backs upon the Church; the rest were more or less estranged from the Church's life.[2] The tiny band of young neo-Christians from all walks of life – factory, field, university – all those, in short, whose hearts have been kindled, are our hope. The prospects of any endeavour are always determined much more by the enthusiasm of its supporters than by their number.

Our earnest care, however, must be directed to the great mass of those who are indeed within the Church into which they were born, but who have never given the slightest thought to what that means. They live as those around them live, and follow their customs as long as these customs are observed. Today the religious practice and the whole life of these Christians of habit is being exposed to many corrosive influences. It is not merely that the rationalism and critical attitude inherited from the philosophical outlook of the nineteenth century have long since set the intellectual tone; it is not merely that the variety of views

[1] P. Hitz, 'Christozentrische Glaubensverkündigung', *Paulus*, XXI, 1949, p. 14.
[2] F. Jantsch in *Wort und Wahrheit*, III, 1948, p. 793.

of the universe and of philosophies of life which spring
up all around us threaten to make everything appear
relative, so that we are tempted to accept everything and
take nothing very seriously. It is more than this: something
which has in fact been a gain from the labours of the past
century – the tremendous insight into the laws of nature
and the structure of the universe – has become a threat to
naïve faith inherited from past generations, for this kind
of faith is unable to distinguish between solid content
and dispensable wrappings. The universe has become
intelligible without reference to God. Only on the very
broadest view, only away on the extreme edge, so to speak,
is there still a riddle pointing towards other spheres: but
everyday thought never penetrates as far as this extreme
edge.

All that life now owes to man's power of discovery plays
its part here. Man today does not see himself as directly
face to face with God-created nature. He lives in a world
devised by man and in which man controls nature. Apart
from border-line cases, which rarely come into view, the
dangerous elements which terrified former generations have
been tamed. True, the world lies under a threat, but it is no
longer a vale of tears. The darkness in which childlike
existence straightway sought and found God has been
almost completely illumined. God has been pushed into
the distance; the Christian message seems to lack the strength
for the logical rethinking that is required, the feasts and
celebrations of the Church no longer serve as a mainstay. The
bells may still ring out in the morning, but this is a mere
poetic glorification of life that would be as little missed
as the punctuation of the now monotonous year by the
regular recurrence of Sunday or the occasional feast-days
of the Church.

For the great bulk of traditionally faithful Christians,

however, the Church's regulation of life continues to be accepted. The Church is still dimly felt to be the representative of a higher power, to be God's ambassador. It would be dangerous to ignore her laws. But are these laws in tune with the realities of modern life? On Sundays and feast-days the faithful are obliged to attend Church for a celebration that is full of obscurities. They are obliged to confess their sins. There are rules of moral conduct which many men of science regard as outmoded. The faithful are asked to believe dogmas that have no foundation in experience, dogmas of the most diverse kinds, indeed, between which there seems to be no recognizable connection. None the less, people are unwilling to risk the loss of their souls. The Church's way still seems the safest way, and at all events the most readily available.

Salvation of the soul, deliverance from the destruction that threatens the sinner – this negative approach causes the most characteristically Christian elements of the faith to fall right into the background. The elements that remain are those that would be valid in a merely natural order, elements that would occur to an intelligent man using his own faculties: the claims of conscience, divine judgement, an after-life in bliss or misery. The elements of Christian revelation and of the order of salvation are simply thrown in as parts of the Church's law – a law that is so all-embracing that people accept it in silence, try to keep it as best they may, but preferring to do without it if that were only possible. No matter how much good-will may be contained in such Christianity, and no matter how adequate it may be for the moment, in the present atmosphere the attitude it presupposes is exceedingly dangerous.

There is undoubtedly a perfectly justifiable form of Christianity which never gains a very deep insight and which devotes all its energy to following the laws laid down by the

Church – an unconscious Christianity.[3] It is a Christianity without enthusiasm, lived in fear and trembling, but none the less with faithful obedience. In the last analysis grace in essence is a free gift which a man has to accept and hold fast, whether he understands what it means or not. Whoever by baptism has received divine sonship and has not destroyed this by sin, or who having done so, following the guidance of the Church, has regained it through the sacrament of penance, will be saved, even though he neither knows how to define the nature of divine sonship nor has any idea of its origin, even though he may never have rejoiced in his good fortune or given thanks for it. So little knowledge of faith is necessary for salvation, that it cannot but be acquired by anyone who somehow or other merely shares in celebrating the feasts of the Church.[4] In the Middle Ages men could be satisfied with such a Christianity. The world around them, public opinion, and a tight net of religious custom saw to it that the individual did not lose contact with the Church and its power to give grace. And so he lived as a Catholic Christian, or if not, almost always died as one.

Today we are not to be comforted by such a hope. In the modern world we rarely find it possible for Christianity to be supported exclusively by our environment. This is even less possible and more risky when Christianity is purely legalistic and joyless. The ballast will be thrown overboard completely as soon as a hard case arises – a marriage problem, the bad example of others, or a political revolution. People are unaware then that they have thrown out the pearl of great price to gain which a man has to give up everything.

Clearly what we must now do is to strengthen the bonds

---

[3] Cf. J. Jungmann, *Pastoral Liturgy*, London, 1962, Part III, Chap. 1, 'Christianity – Conscious or Unconscious?'

[4] Cf. St Thomas Aquinas, *De veritate*, q. 14, a. 11.

that are threatening to break. This task can be approached from below, starting, that is, from human nature. For Christianity, however much it is grace – the free gift of the divine goodness – is nevertheless no stranger to human nature. On the contrary, human nature is so designed that it must always be open towards God, not just towards his revelation in the silence of nature, but also towards the word that he may possibly utter. Conversely we need not be amazed if God, having crowned the wonders of nature with the creation of the human spirit, should come to meet this spirit and address it through a historical word, should in fact begin to take up a dialogue with it. It is also important to establish this basic congruence between human nature and revelation. This congruence goes beyond mere demonstration that the human intellect unassisted by revelation can only with great difficulty acquire sufficient knowledge of God and of divine things; it establishes man's moral need of revelation.[5]

In what follows attention will be directed to the careful presentation of the subject from the divine angle. The substance of the faith must be presented not as though it were a casual collection of arbitrary details, but so as to come alive in its wholeness and power. The Christian message did indeed come into the world as good news,

[5] In doing this we must not fall into the trap of asserting that God must of necessity reveal himself to intelligent beings once he has created them. As is well known, Pius XII denied this in his encyclical *Humani generis*, *A.A.S.*, XLII, 1950, p. 570. We cannot assume that man possesses a *potential positiva* for grace, because that would be to merge grace into mere nature. On the other hand we must not define the *potentia obedientalis*, which simply denotes the capacity to be addressed by God, in such a way as to signify nothing more than the mere absence of contradiction between nature and grace. Cf. Karl Rahner, *Nature and Grace*, London, 1963, p. 41: 'Going into all this in order to try and get a metaphysical anthropology as close as possible to the teaching on grace and to see the higher as the gratuitous fulfilment of the lower, is not just idle playing about. If we don't do this it will not be possible in the long run to awaken in people an existential interest in that mysterious life which is given in supernatural grace.' We refer also in this connection to the same author's conception of the supernatural existential in *Lexikon für Theologie und Kirche*,[2] III, 1959, p. 1301.

and the Christmas angels sang with a joy that was meant not just for a chosen few but for all people. In the life of the Church, too, there have been periods when joy over the treasure that man has found was so much the underlying mood, not merely of individuals or a group, but of the whole Christian population, that readiness for martyrdom was taken for granted. These were times when, as has been said, every serious professor of the faith handed it on in such good measure that when Christianity finally prevailed in the Roman empire it could be said that 'the great mission of Christianity was in reality accomplished by means of informal missionaries.'[6] It should be possible, therefore, for the mass of the faithful to profess a Christianity that is not a burdensome drag upon their lives, but a source of joyous pride. In our preaching of Christianity there must be something that goes beyond the reinvigoration and intensified application of the traditional forms of sermon, catechesis, and worship. It will at least be worth while to look more closely into the content and structure of the word of God, and test possibilities which have not perhaps been sufficiently exploited in this field.

Fundamentally we face the problem of how far the power of impact of the Christian message can be increased by a more logical concentration in its presentation. In the Epistle to the Hebrews (4. 12) we read: 'For the word of God is living and active, sharper than any two-edged sword.' It is also repeatedly described as a well-defined entity, as the Word, as a message, as good news, as the announcement of salvation, as the Way, as something which, if need be, can be expressed in few words, which a man always keeps before his eyes, always bears as a light in his heart, always takes as his life's compass. Cardinal Suhard, in a famous pastoral to catechists, makes this very point. 'Catechists

---

[6] A. Harnack, *The Mission and Expansion of Christianity*, London, 1904, p. 460.

and Christian teachers must never be allowed to make the mistake of presenting the Christian faith in isolated pieces. Do not dismember your message on the pretext of logic or necessity. . . . Do not kill it by triviality. Go straight to the heart of the mystery. Do not hold back souls without cause but plunge them straight into the life of Christ and of the Church.'[7]

These words describe the programme everywhere accepted today by the best minds. The programme must, however, be repeatedly stressed and if possible further explained and more profoundly based. In spite of all our dependence upon the crowd, the whole cultural mood of the age is against the acceptance of unintelligible demands. In political and technical life ordinary men are regarded as having a fair degree of competence; in religion, too, people want to be treated as responsible adults. In his religious life the one who listens must now be credited with a certain intellectual autonomy.

Our task is no longer simply to proclaim the separate demands of Christianity, through the fulfilment of which salvation may be won. A hundred years ago, Deharbe's catechism traced the whole content of Christian doctrine back to three duties: we must believe, keep the commandments, and use the means of grace. This was never a very happy conception. Today it would be doubly mistaken, because it corresponds neither to the nature of the good news God offers us, nor to the psychological make-up of man. It has therefore rightly been abandoned.

It is not the demands, not the separate commandments which must be placed in the foreground, but the divine plan from which the commandments arise. As has been said: every imperative must proceed from an indicative. In the Gospel account itself the call to repentance is founded upon

[7] Cardinal Suhard in the quarterly *Documentation catéchistique.*

the message: the Kingdom of Heaven is at hand: and at Pentecost, before Peter called the crowd to repentance and baptism he recalled to them the divine plan of salvation, from the predictions of the prophets to the resurrection of the Redeemer. So today we must build up in those who want to listen to us an understanding and conscious Christianity, the demands of which will be willingly and gladly accepted, because they grow out of an insight into the order which God has decreed, and because this order graciously fulfils the noblest longings of our souls. If we do this, then the content of that which we preach as the order of God, as religious truth, will not appear as a disconnected miscellany, precisely because it will be preached as the message about a way that God has prepared for us, the way of salvation leading through this world, and ending in nothing less than a share in the life of the Blessed Trinity.

Such concentration upon essentials is in harmony with the trend of the times, a trend expressed nowhere more clearly than in modern architecture. Every detail of a building is subordinated to its function. Extraneous decoration is left out. This applies to sacred as well as profane buildings. Likewise in the devotional life of the faithful, of those who truly lead a life of prayer, a profound change has occurred. The prayer book, with its plethora of badly arranged sentimental texts, which held the field fifty years ago, has now been largely supplanted by the Church's missal.

Above all, however, it is in the teaching of the faith that a mighty step forward has been accomplished along a similar direction. This is very plainly seen in the new catechism for the German dioceses published in 1955.[8] Not only has this work freed itself from Deharbe's groundplan of a catechism as the enumeration of all that a man must do, thus giving prominence to what God has done;

[8] *A Catholic Catechism*, London, 1957 – English translation of above.

it has also succeeded in once again allowing this action of God to become visible as the one work of salvation that is being accomplished through Christ and in his Church. One of the most important tasks of present-day pastoral theology and practical pastoral endeavour is to follow up this line of thought even more logically and assist the ripening in all fields of the salutary fruits of such labours. There are many points, particularly in the sphere of preaching and devotional life, upon which reflexion and examination are required, so that what is valuable in our heritage of forms and formulae, of customs and practices, shall not thoughtlessly be abandoned, and also so that ballast which could be replaced by something better shall not be unnecessarily preserved. It is not, after all, a question of making a completely fresh start, but of fitting the existing parts properly into the whole, into the picture of the new divine order, of establishing this picture as an unchanging background and fixed framework for the multifarious searchings and struggles that pass across the stage of life, Christian life in particular.

We can describe this totality in various ways. It is salvation-history, begun in the old covenant, reaching its climax in the fullness of time and continuing in the history of the Church until the second coming of our Lord. St Paul calls it the mystery hidden in God before the beginning of time, but now revealed to his saints.[9] He calls it God's decree, or plan, the purpose of which is to gather together in Christ all things that are in heaven and on earth (Eph. 1. 10). Elsewhere this totality appears as God's gracious call (κλῆσις: Eph. 1. 18; 4. 1, etc.) to the human race, or as the assembly (ἐκκλησία) of those who have heard and obeyed

---

[9] Col. 1. 26; Rom. 16. 26; Eph. 3. 5. For a superb exposition of this Pauline concept see L. Bouyer, *Liturgical Piety*, Notre Dame, Indiana, 1955, pp. 99–114, 143–271.

the call – the holy Church. Our Lord's parables teach us to speak of the kingdom of God that has come to us, or to take up one of the images in which this kingdom is portrayed, above all the image of the great wedding feast of the king who sends out his messengers to invite the guests, the picture which simultaneously portrays divine grace and, in warning, fatal human rejection of it.

In every case, however, the person of Christ stands at the centre – the climax of salvation-history, the 'messenger of the great plan,' the Word of God, the call that has gone out to the world, the Lord and King of those who are called and whom he leads home into the kingdom of his Father. In this way is the order of religious reality described: it is an objective Christocentricity that is given in divine revelation, quite independent of our minds. Today this must be matched by a corresponding subjective Christocentricity. That is to say, in the preaching of the faith and in the awareness of the believer not only must separate doctrines and ideas arising from the objective Christian message recur more or less faithfully, but Christ himself must assume his place therein as the centre-point, as the source of light from which all other doctrinal points are brightly illumined.

As already indicated, this requirement is not absolute. As in a healthy environment a solid habitual Christianity is by no means impossible, so there are circumstances in which a preaching of the faith is possible which contents itself with making known the more important doctrinal propositions and commandments, while paying no further heed to their interconnexions. It is only under conditions such as we know today that the Christocentric arrangement in preaching the faith becomes an absolute obligation. The requirement of Christocentricity has in any case found almost universal acceptance in the last few decades. We might even say that it dominates not only pastoral theology, but also the greater part of all religious literature. Nevertheless, the fresh wind now blowing has still to penetrate many neglected corners, so further study is still required; and most advantage will come from study that approaches the subject historically.

II

The Origin

WE DO not have to prove but merely to point out that the preaching of the faith in the early Church was of the utmost simplicity. It contained merely the good news of the salvation which God offered to men through Christ. We have only to read St Paul and note the constant background to all his changing themes, the facts which, prophesied of old, he assumes to be well known, which he specially emphasizes, and which form the single motif behind all his teaching: Christ died for us sinners, was buried, and rose again on the third day (I Cor. 15. 3 f.), that in baptism we have risen with him (Rom. 6. 3 ff.) and become members of his body the Church (Rom. 12. 5; I Cor. 12. 12 ff.), and that now our task is to remain faithful to what has been given us (Phil. 4. 1), and to lead a life 'in Christ,' so that when he returns as judge we may be able to pass the test (Rom. 2. 16). We find an even more primitive sketch of the first preaching in the sermons of the Acts of the Apostles – St Peter's sermon to Cornelius, for example (Acts 10. 34 ff.): Jesus of Nazareth was anointed by the Holy Spirit, was nailed upon the cross, and killed, but God raised him from the dead; we are offered forgiveness of sins in his name. It is nothing short of amazing how little knowledge was expected of those who received the word and were baptized.[1] At first preaching sought only to place the supernatural epiphany of Christ before people's eyes, to arouse their enthusiasm for him, and so bring about a decision for him, and hence faith.

[1] Cf. A. Rétif, *Foi au Christ et mission d'après les Actes des Apôtres*, Paris, 1953, pp. 97 ff.

It is true that a catechesis appeared in which these doctrines were further developed (Gal. 6. 6). The Gospels may correctly be regarded as the recording of such further development. In them the account of the crucified and risen Lord was extended at one end by a demonstration of the miraculous power and divine origin of him who had risen, and at the other by references to the continuing life of the risen Lord and to his second coming.[2] At all times, however, it remains the message about a fact, about the decisive phase in the history of man's salvation, in which all that happened (*secundum Scripturas*) had been anticipated in the Old Testament as preparatory history or prefiguration. Even when concerned with moral demands we seldom find St Paul appealing for motive to the material, created order; he points rather to Christ, to the salvation given in him, to the calling which is ours through him.[3] The same way of looking at things is displayed in the document which might be called the oldest Christian catechism: the Apostles' Creed. Here, too, the chief section of this brief outline of Christian doctrine is made up of the Christ-kerygma, the sketch of salvation history, of the work of our redemption, beginning with the entry of God's Son into the world, made decisively real in his death on the cross 'under Pontius Pilate,' and consummated in the Resurrection and Ascension and his eternal kingship at the right hand of the Father. Here, in the form of a summary of more expanded catechesis, the framework is fixed into which the historical account is fitted: the order linking God and his

---

[2] Cf. R. Schnackenburg in his contribution to the symposium *Fragen der Theologie heute*, Einsiedeln, 1957, pp. 151 f.: 'In the primitive Church there was a common foundation of preaching – the original apostolic kerygma. We see this at its most concise in I Cor. 15. 3–5, expanded in the missionary sermons of the Acts of the Apostles, and it provides the framework for the Gospels.' Cf. also H. Schürmann, *Aufbau und Struktur der neutestamentilchen Verkündigung*, Paderborn, 1949.

[3] Cf. L. Nieder, *Die Motive der religiös-sittlichen Paränese in den paulinischen Gemeindebriefen*, Munich, 1956, especially pp. 144 f.

world, from which the work of redemption proceeds, against the background, indeed, of the Blessed Trinity – Father, Son, and Holy Spirit.[4] The world is the work of the one God who has revealed himself as Father; Christ himself is the only-begotten of the Father; the Trinity is completed by the Holy Spirit who fills the Church in which the faithful are cleansed from sin and prepared for the resurrection and eternal life.

The structure of the creed exactly corresponds to the liturgical celebration of the early Church. At the centre once more we find a fact of redemption expressed in its triumphal climax – the Resurrection; and, what is more, from the very start this central fact was celebrated, not only at Easter, but week by week on Sunday, most likely even before any special Easter festival had been inaugurated. Preparation was made for Sunday by fasting on Friday (and Wednesday), and from at least the third century onwards this fast was associated with commemoration of our Lord's passion. Thus Easter, as the *triduum crucifixi, sepulti, suscitati*, is but the more elaborate annual celebration of the same event. From the fourth century onwards Christmas, separated by several months from Easter, began to be celebrated as the feast of our Lord's entry into this world – *natus ex Maria Virgine*; and gradually the concluding feast of the Easter cycle began to be clearly distinguished as the separate feast of the outpouring of the Holy Spirit upon the Church – *Credo in Spiritum Sanctum, sanctam Ecclesiam*. From the earliest times, as at all times, the celebration was essentially that of the Eucharist, a sacrifice of praise and thanksgiving to God, in which, persisting from the very earliest times, we find one and the same fundamental note.

---

[4] The 'triadic' scheme as a summary of the whole catechesis probably existed from the start alongside the Christ-kerygma. Cf. J. N. D. Kelly, *Early Christian Creeds*, London, 1950, pp. 52, 71 ff., etc.; A. Stenzel, *Die Taufe*, Innsbruck, 1958, pp. 81 f.

Hippolytus of Rome is already using the words in which, following the command to repeat this act, the meaning of the celebration is described: *memores igitur passionis et resurrectionis eius*. Primarily the Eucharist is *anamnesis*, just as a Christian feast is essentially *anamnesis* – commemoration.

Along with the Eucharist the Church guards another great treasure: the Scriptures. It is instructive to note how the Old Testament was used in patristic times. It was accepted with reverence as the word of God, and zealously used; but people showed little interest in its literal meaning, in the details of this ancient preparation. Wherever possible the events and regulations, down to the detailed ritual prescriptions of the Book of Leviticus, were all interpreted as adumbrations of that one event which in the fullness of time completely effected our redemption.[5]

In particular the Book of Psalms was not only read diligently, but very early, since the third century at the latest, it was taken as the Church's prayerbook. From the start the psalms were seen in the light of the New Testament and read with Christian eyes. It would be quite easy to dig out from St Augustine's *Enarrationes in psalmos* – his commentary on all 150 psalms – the whole of Christian doctrine and all the mysteries of the new covenant. This viewpoint controlled exegesis of the psalms during the early centuries.[6] The same essential attitude is represented by St Athanasius when he explains that many psalms, in some way or other, speak of Christ, either by announcing his coming or by being his mouthpiece.[7]

Certainly this way of regarding the psalms is the only thing which explains why this Old Testament book became the Church's first prayerbook, and why it has maintained

[5] J. Daniélou, *Sacramentum futuri*, Paris, 1950.
[6] B. Fischer, *Die Psalmenfrömmigkeit der Märtyrerkirche*, Freiburg, 1949.
[7] *Ep. ad Marcellinum*, n. 609 (*P. G.* XXVII, 15–20).

this position. At any rate in the early Middle Ages the psalms were still very much alive in this sense. This fact is vividly impressed upon us by the collection of psalm-titles in early medieval manuscript psalters, which we owe to the Benedictines who produced editions of the Vulgate.[8] There are six different series of such titles, and all agree in their effort to place these hymns of the Old Testament bard under the light of the redemptive facts of the New Testament. One of these series, the fifth, makes every title begin with the words: *quod ipse* (*Christus*). The first psalm shows that he (*quod ipse*) is the tree of life, the second that he has received all nations of the earth as an inheritance from his Father, the third that he has known the sleep of death for our sakes and has risen again, etc. The other series of titles are very much the same. In the psalm they detect references to the passion or the victory of Christ, to the calling of the nations, and to the new people of God. In the psalm they hear the *vox Christi* or the *vox Ecclesiae*, or even the voice of the apostles proclaiming the new covenant, or the voice of the faithful praising God for this. It was thus a strictly circumscribed cycle of thought which filled the mind of early Christians; but it was reflected in a wealth of imagery and forms and thus was bound to stir the heart and impress the mind all the more powerfully.

There is definitely a reflexion of this mood and mentality in the austere mural paintings of the catacombs, where the Christian hope beyond the grave found expression in recurring pictures of rescue and redemption; for all of these pictures are upon this theme: Noah in the ark, Daniel in the lions' den, Susanna and her persecutors, the water gushing from the rock, the rescue of Jonas, the raising of Lazarus, the healing of the paralytic. All these events, as the literary evidence states more specifically, denote the

[8] P. Salmon, *Les tituli psalmorum des manuscrits latins*, Rome, 1959.

decisive redemption, the resurrection of Christ and the resurrection along with him of all who believe in him. The same thought is expressed even more plainly in the prominent portrayal of the Good Shepherd. He is portrayed carrying the sheep he has saved – mankind – upon his shoulders, or with sheep clustered confidently around him.

In sharper focus still we see the same decisive motif taking its place in the apse mosaics of the basilicas where the glorified Christ appears as the law-giver, surrounded by his apostles, and with the holy city, Jerusalem, as background. Sometimes the picture is of a radiant cross upon mount Sion. The rivers of paradise flow from it, and harts quench their thirst in the waters; or the abundant foliage of the sacred vine entwines the cross, and doves feed on the grapes.

It is true that very soon numerous other motifs appeared within the Church, but it is significant how the portrayal of the facts which are the Church's faith and hope firmly retained the place to which the eye of the worshipper was always turned – the space above the altar.

Obviously, as has been well known for a long time, many elements in the idiom of early Christian art were taken over from classical artistic tradition: spring landscapes, vines, hart and dove, pastoral scenes, and even the shepherd who carries the sheep.[9] It is worth noting, however, that even whole series of pictures from classical life and poetry were reinterpreted to fit the Christian mysteries. Hugo Rahner has drawn attention to numerous examples of such pictorial language. The sun that sinks in the evening, passes through the underworld, and rises radiant in the morning, becomes an image of the Redeemer who dies, descends to the fathers, and rises in glory; the moon that acquires new life in its encounter with the sun at new moon and then grows until it becomes the full moon, is an image of the Church. The

[9] T. Klauser in *Jahrbuch f. Antike und Christentum*, 1, 1958, pp. 33–7, 45 f.

Christian is able to sail safely across the sea of this life only if the mast of the cross is erected in his ship, and the breath of the Holy Spirit fills the sails. In fact, just as Odysseus had himself bound to the mast and his ears stopped to avoid becoming ensnared by the song of the sirens, so the Christian must stick fast to his Lord's cross and become deaf to the enticements of the world. But he can take heart: the ship in which he sails is the Church which will be safely steered by her pilot into the haven of eternal life.

It is true that disruptive tendencies began at an early stage to affect the understanding of the Christian message. Heathen memories played their part in popular piety, for example in the cult of the dead. Gnosticism, too, with its fantastic genealogies and speculations, pressed into the ranks of the Christian people, as is shown by widely circulated New Testament apocrypha, especially the histories of the apostles. Very early, the veneration of martyrs assumed forms which passed the bounds of true proportion. Notwithstanding these things, the Church's preaching through doctrine and worship remained true to the broad outlines of the Christian message, and so impressed the faithful, that even the average Christian knew what it was that he possessed by faith, and expressed his joy and pride in it by a cheerful disposition.

III

Disruptive Forces

FIRST AND foremost Christianity is a fact – the intervention of God in the history of the human race. Only in a secondary sense is it doctrine, the announcement of that fact in words – a message. This message too has been proclaimed within the history of mankind. At first it was heard by a particular race, and found expression in human language; then it had to be handed on in human language from race to race and from generation to generation. Hence that which is timeless and divine became in many ways tarnished by that which is changeable and human. And so the message found a primary regulative expression in the particular conceptual world of its messengers. Indeed, we have come to speak of a Jewish–Christian theology. Later, the Greek spirit, with its clarity and tidy concepts, deeply influenced Christian doctrine; and the Latin sense of order, too, made its contribution.

At an early date the Christian message encountered opposition, not merely the outward opposition of persecution, but also the intellectual opposition of human philosophy, which, unable to grasp the colossal fact of Christianity, tried to reduce the message of the Gospel to fit human norms, thus producing heresies – truncated forms of the Gospel. Resistance to heresy thus became a decisive factor in the development of the Christian message. Heresy could never survive did it not contain elements of the truth which it exaggerates and distorts at the expense of other elements, and by means of which it allures men. Consequently the Church is compelled to defend and stress the neglected elements of the truth. This stress leads almost inevitably to a temporary disturbance of equilibrium, to an alteration in the pattern of the message. The most violent disturbances of this sort were caused by the Christological heresies of the second half of the early Christian period, and the anti-Arian counterblast of the following periods.

Finally, since the high Middle Ages the enquiring mind of man has been hard at work – especially in scholasticism – trying more and more to extend the sphere of knowledge of the truth disclosed through the word of God by a synthesis with philosophical premises, to develop the interpretation of the message of Christ into a comprehensive theology, a genuine doctrine of God, to erect it into a mighty system, and thus at the same time to assure it in advance against the attacks of critical reason. There can be no doubt that this has been a great gain, but at the same time it has produced a new temptation, even in preaching the faith, to concentrate on a multitude of isolated pieces of knowledge, to exalt knowledge above its due, and so to obscure the true message concerning the facts of salvation-history. This temptation was not sufficiently resisted by the average preacher at the close of the Middle Ages, nor by the authors of the catechisms of the eighteenth and nineteenth centuries. Today it is becoming ever clearer that the primary and authentic form of manifestation of God's word that is entrusted to the Church is not the scientific elaboration of the word, but its transmission in teaching through sermon, catechesis, mission, writing, liturgy.[1] Within the organism of the Church theology is above all an organ of consolidation, admittedly of immense importance; but it is only as consolidation, as a prevention against straying, a bulwark

[1] Cf. V. Schurr, 'Situation und Aufgabe der Predigt heute' in *Verkündigung und Glaube*, Freiburg, 1958, p. 199: 'The word of God in the sermon is God addressing us. . . . That is to say the sermon, not science, is the primitive and authentic thing in Christianity.' If Schurr does not attribute the same status to catechesis that is probably because he has in mind catechesis that is simply bare instruction.

against assailing errors, that it can also be a norm of teaching.

If, then, many factors have exerted a modifying, formative, and even disruptive, effect upon the original message, it follows that there must be a place for critical examination; for it is possible that here and there a development which seemed to signify progress will have to be reversed, in short, that in the field of the preaching of the faith reforms may now fall due.

It need not surprise us if we meet the objection that in such an important sphere of the Church's life as the preaching and teaching of the faith the question of reform cannot possibly arise, that the actual developments which have taken place must be recognized as the guidance of the Holy Spirit, that a return, even partial, to early Christian forms and models is but mistaken archaeologism.

This objection must be taken seriously. It is an essential endowment of the Church to be the 'pillar and foundation of the truth.' This does not, however, prevent faults emerging in the way in which the truth is proclaimed. The Church is indeed holy, but this holiness does not exclude manifold human inadequacies from her life. There would, of course, be no question at all of reforms in the Church, were it not that from time to time these human inadequacies make themselves felt in peripheral matters. At the same time we have to affirm that these inadequacies are not all on the side of the members, but are to be found also in the weaknesses of the leadership of the Church, in their narrowness of vision, their faint-heartedness, their too great or too little adaptation to the demands of the time, in attitudes, that is, which are simply a consequence of the limitations of human endowment, and which may not even be culpable. We must be all the more prepared for such inadequacy, for even culpable weakness in the leadership of the Church is by no means excluded.[2] All too frequently Church history has to record, in small things and in great, directives, acts of condonement, even legislation, which sooner or later have been proved unfortunate if not wrong. We need only recall the entrenched system of benefices in the later Middle Ages, the reservations and expectations, the plurality of benefices, and so on.[3] Even more doubtful practices, such as the *oblatio puerorum* with obligation to enter the religious life, or the case of the death-penalty in the ecclesiastical sphere, even though administered by the secular arm, may be understood but not justified in the light of the circumstances of the time.

There is a topic which stands closer to our problem of the teaching of the faith – the first communion of children. On this subject we have an important document of Pope Pius X, which speaks of the *haud pauci errores plorandique abusus*, which had crept in concerning the age at which first communion ought to be received.[4] This document condemns a practice which for several centuries had been regarded as the norm in the Western Church, had been prescribed as such by synods,[5] and which the supreme authority in the Church had not bothered to contest.

We can raise very little objection to an expert on the causes of the Reformation who prefaces his observations with the affirmation that the objective truth and holiness of the Church is subject to no variation, but goes on to say:

[2] Cf. Karl Rahner, 'Die Kirche der Sünder' in *Stimmen der Zeit*, CXL, 1947, pp. 163–77; p. 170: 'If the concept of the Church is not to evaporate into an abstract ideal of an invisible Church, then there can be no dogma which states that the assistance of the Holy Spirit, always present in the Church, restricts the influence of human sinfulness in the leadership of the Church to their private lives, keeping quite unsullied that activity which has to be unequivocally described as the action of the Church.'

[3] I. Zeiger, *Historia iuris canonici*, II, Rome, 1940, p. 18, speaks of *leges vel consuetudines . . . in se quidem honestae . . . quae ad finem Ecclesiae spiritualem parum conducant, imo sequelas funestas adducere queant.*

[4] *A.A.S.,* II, 1910, p. 579.

[5] Cf. P. Browe, *Die Pflichtkommunion im Mittelalter*, Münster, 1940, pp. 160–77.

'But this holiness and this possession of the truth are rigidly limited to the sacraments and to dogma in the strict sense. Short of this, absolutely everything in the Church is exposed to weakness, abuse, and corruption.'[6]

The purpose of these remarks is simply to make plain that even in the history of preaching and teaching the faith there occur possibilities of variation, of versions of the heritage of faith which in one respect or another are imperfect and deficient, or at least conditioned by their own time, so that they are insufficient for later ages. It is the last of these possibilities that requires closest attention. Religious things and even the linguistic formulations of religious ideas always tend, once they have been fixed, to be held in special reverence over long periods of time. As early as the twelfth century Peter Cantor was complaining of the 'burden and the profusion of traditions.'[7] It may very well happen that a usage, a formulary, is well adapted to the needs of one age, but is no longer adequate for the altered presuppositions and requirements of a later age.

This is a fact which we shall be able to establish many times over within this very sphere of the preaching of the faith.

---

[6] J. Lortz, *Wie kam es zur Reformation?*, Einsiedeln, 1950, p. 30. On the limits to the assistance of the Holy Spirit in the Church cf. Ch. Journet, *L'Église du Verbe. Incarné*, I, Paris, 1941, pp. 397–462.

[7] *Verbum abbreviatum*, c. 79 (P. L. CCV, 233–9): *Contra traditionum onerositatem et multitudinem* (title).

IV

Christological Developments

TODAY, threatened on all sides, the preaching of the faith is forced in a special way to concentrate its energies, to become Christocentric. Quite obviously, therefore, we shall take a keen interest in all developments touching on this decisive point. The fourth century saw the mighty battle over the dogma of Christ. The repercussions of this continued into later centuries. The very necessary defensive attack upon the teaching of Arius, who denied true divinity to Christ and wanted to see the Son of God as no more than the highest creature, resulted in a concentration of attention upon the person of our Lord, and upon the precise definition of his nature. Early Christianity, like the New Testament, had regularly spoken of Christ as he appears in salvation-history, as Redeemer, the Good Shepherd, the Head of the Church, the bringer of salvation. Even the prologue to St John's Gospel, which lays such great stress upon the dignity of the divine Word, simply adds: 'But to all who received him, who believed in his name, he gave power to become children of God.' The names and titles, even those presenting images from the Old Testament, regularly show him as the bringer of salvation. Christology and soteriology formed a unity. In the fourth century this unity fell into the background. In controversy the point assailed had to be defended, had, to some extent, to become isolated.[1] The great councils fixed the definitive outlines of

[1] Cf. J. Ratzinger, 'Christozentrik in der Verkündigung' in *Trierer theol. Zeitschrift*, LXX, 1961, pp. 1–14; p. 2: 'Theological discussion of the concept of the Logos, and, in general, the dialogue between Christianity and Greek philosophy, led gradually to a shift of interest from the historical to the ontological, from the

the doctrine of Christ: the consubstantiality of the Son with the Father (Nicaea 325); the unity of the person of Christ in two natures, the divine and the human (Ephesus 431); the relationship of the two natures to one another, joined so as to be unconfused yet unseparated (Chalcedon 451).

So violent was this strife, affecting the very nerve-centre of Christianity, that it soon spread out beyond the sphere of intellectual activity and took hold of every sphere of Church life, especially that of public worship. This was specially true in the East. In that part of the world it was customary for every solemn prayer by bishop or priest to end in a doxology. The forms which these doxologies had acquired followed the same underlying scheme: glory be to God through Christ in the Holy Spirit; or, stressing the mystery of the Trinity even more strongly: glory be to the Father through the Son in the Holy Spirit. It was this latter formula which became the battleground. The Arians claimed it for themselves because it clearly expressed the subordination of the Son to the Father. The Catholics were not content to insist that the expression 'through the Son' referred to Christ, the God-man, who in respect of his manhood was indeed subordinate to the Father, but not in respect of his divinity. The Catholics countered the Arians with another confessional formula, which in any case had long been traditional among the Syrians. This was: glory be to the Father, and to the Son, and to the Holy Spirit. This formula removed all ambiguity, and is the one still current with us today.

The well-known case of Bishop Leontius of Antioch in about A.D. 350 shows how violently passions were aroused by this controversy. This bishop, wishing to offend no

work of Christ to his person. This facilitated a needed theological clarification, but at the same time introduced a shift of the centre of gravity which might lead, and here and there did lead, along the wrong road.'

B

party, was compelled to say the words of the doxology so
softly that even those nearest to him could hear only the
concluding phrase 'for ever and ever.'[2] The deep penetration of this strife into liturgical life in another Eastern
metropolis, Caesarea, is revealed in the writings of Basil.
In the version of the Eucharistic Prayer used in that city,
whenever Christ is named, his divinity is stressed; and
there is scarcely any mention of his humanity and its
significance for redemption. Basil likewise lays great stress
upon the sense of remoteness from, and trembling awe
before, the eternal God, Christ, and his judgement. At all
events it is significant that the fear and awe which today
surrounds the mention of the Eucharist in the Eastern
liturgies first made its appearance in Basil and the Greek
Fathers who followed him.[3] As they migrated westwards
from the Byzantine empire, the Teutonic tribes brought
Arianism with them. Whereas in other places they had been
content to allow Arianism to distinguish them in religion
from the indigenous Catholic populations, in other places –
North Africa and Spain – not only did physical persecution
at times result, but theological controversy as well. As in
the East, so too in the Western Catholic Church it was this
controversy rather than persecution which made a permanent mark upon devotional attitudes.[4] For a confessional
formula signifying conversion to Arianism, King Leovigild
of the Visigoths (d. 586) demanded simply the doxology:
'Glory be to the Father through the Son in the Holy Spirit.'
Consequently, on the Catholic side, any formula, no matter
how Catholic, if, like this doxology, it appeared to subordinate the Son to the Father, was sedulously avoided.

[2] Theodoret, *Hist. eccl.* II, 24.

[3] This fact has been much discussed since E. Bishop (d. 1917). The origin of the
mode of thought (φρικτός, φοβερός, φρικωδέστατος is predicated of the Eucharist)
has not been fully explained. Cf. the reference to the state of the discussion in J. A.
Jungmann, *Die Stellung Christi im liturgischen Gebet*[2], Münster, 1962, pp. XXI* f.

[4] J. A. Jungmann, *Pastoral Liturgy*, London, 1962, pp. 23-32.

The old Spanish liturgy uses the *per Christum* in its older strata, but the more modern sections avoid it. The form of address in prayer likewise is no longer regularly directed to God the Father, as was prescribed for public worship by North African synods in the fourth century, but became deliberately directed now to the Son, now to the Father, now to the Blessed Trinity, so as to exclude all suspicion of a denial of the divinity of Christ or any misinterpretation of the mystery of the Trinity. The doggedness with which the synods of Toledo circumscribed the confession of the Blessed Trinity in ever new formulae is well known.[5]

At first these events of the fifth and sixth centuries appear to represent developments purely in the realm of the history of dogma, only affecting the surface of doctrine and a narrowly delimited sphere of liturgical forms within a single country. In reality these were the events which provided the stimulus for that development in intellectual and religious life which gave the Middle Ages a stamp so different from that of the world of the Fathers. This was a slow process of fermentation lasting for centuries, an evolutionary stream which received many tributaries in its later course. The origin of the process in the resistance to Arian attacks, and the consequent importance of the part played by Spain, are well illustrated by the history of the Creed of the Mass – known, significantly, as the Nicaeo-Constantinopolitan Creed. The sharply anti-heretical phrasing of this creed seemed to make it particularly useful as a profession of Catholic faith in times of battle with Arianism. With this end in view it was introduced into the Byzantine Mass about A.D. 500. It appeared a century later in the West, first of all in Spain in 589 when the Visigoth nation renounced Arianism. We can then trace its progress to Ireland and England, whence it travelled further with Alcuin to the

[5] Denzinger, *Enchiridion*, n. 275 ff., 294 ff.

imperial court chapel of Charlemagne, and finally, through
the mediation of the German Emperor Henry II, to Rome
where it was adopted in the Roman Mass in 1014. Today it
is an accepted fact that in the tenth and eleventh centuries
many and various institutions in law and in the general
sphere of Church order, as well as liturgical institutions
and attitudes, travelled south from the Franco-German
realm.[6] With regard to teaching the faith it is enough to
refer to the fact that at that time in Rome the ancient
traditional Roman form of the Apostles' Creed gave way to
the native Gallican form, the so-called *Textus receptus*
(which among other things contains the interpolations
descendit ad inferos, sanctorum communionem).

That an intellectual-religious revolution occurred some
time between the decline of Christian antiquity and the high
Middle Ages, is plain for all to see. Attempts have been
made to explain this revolution in terms of the gradually
accomplished dominance of the Teutonic mentality after
the migration of the peoples, a dominance which found
later artistic expression in the emergence of Gothic civilization.[7] St Bernard in particular has sometimes been
regarded as the first representative of the new mode of
thought,[8] and some have wanted to date the actual transition
at the turn of the eleventh and twelfth centuries. This later
date may be justified if we are thinking of the maturity of
the new mentality; but the decisive changes were taking
place much earlier. They had already been accomplished in
the period of the Carolingian renaissance. It was merely the
effects, the practical consequences, which required time to
reach their goal – like the migration of the Creed, which

[6] T. Klauser, 'Die liturgischen Austauschbeziehungen zwischen der römischen
und der fränkisch-deutschen Kirche vom 8. bis zum 11. Jahrhundert' in *Hist.
Jahrbuch*, LIII, 1933, pp. 169–89.

[7] I. Herwegen, *Kirche und Seele*, Münster, 1926, p. 15 ff.

[8] W. Kahles, *Radbert und Bernhard. Zwei Ausprägungen christlicher Frömmigkeit*,
Emsdetten, 1938.

we have mentioned. These consequences are to be seen very plainly in the fifteen Carolingian model catecheses, traditionally regarded as sermons of St Boniface.[9] In these the stress upon the divinity of Christ has gone so far that many phrases express no distinction at all between God and Christ. It is God who was born of the virgin Mary, who endured insults and scourging for us; it was almighty God who entered this world to avert damnation from us; it was our creator, Jesus Christ our Lord, who will lead us to eternal joy. It may well be that besides the repercussions of the anti-Arian attitude a certain naïve simplification of the message of the faith is at work, accommodating the faith to the primitive mentality of the Teutonic tribes; but the facts are obvious. German sermons of the tenth and eleventh centuries unhesitatingly speak of God as eating and drinking with his disciples, of God's feet, of God's passion, and so on.[10] A little later Berthold of Regensburg (d. 1272) liked to speak of the Eucharist as God's body, a manner of speech that persists to this day in the French name 'fête-Dieu,' and the German name 'Herrgottstag' for the feast of Corpus Christi. The same thing applies today to the popular way of speaking about our Lord God upon the Cross, or when a celebrated crucifix is referred to as 'the great God,' or a pilgrimage to the suffering Saviour is called 'God's distress.' These are perfectly orthodox ways of speaking, for they flow from the *communicatio idiomatum*; and they are based upon circumstances in which there was need to stress the divine dignity of the Incarnate. To be true to the kerygma, however, we must preserve also the awareness that this illumines only one side of the mystery of Christ.

Such a way of speaking need not imply that the humanity

[9] Migne, *P. L.* LXXXIX, 843–72. Cf. Jungmann, *Pastoral Liturgy*, London, 1962, pp. 36 f, 43 f.
[10] R. Cruel, *Geschichte der deutschen Predigt im Mittelalter*, Detmold, 1879.

of Christ is bound to be forgotten. Shortly after the turn
of the millennium a type of devotion appeared having as its
definite object the earthly life of our Lord. Thus a broad
field was opened up to contemplation and real edification,
and has remained open until our own day. We must ask,
however, whether in this the humanity of our Lord does
not frequently suffer a reduction in the imagination of the
faithful. Even today we see things which prove that this is
a serious question. The guess was made that if a questionnaire were sent out asking whether or not Jesus had a
human soul, more than half of those asked would say
'No.'[11] The test was made and, in France at least, the guess
proved correct.[12] This conception of the psychology of
Jesus represents the undetected persistence of the heresy
of Apollinarius, an early form of monophysitism that was
condemned by the Council of Chalcedon. This heresy
affirms that in the Incarnation the Logos assumed only the
flesh, the Logos himself taking the place of the soul, so
that the omnipotence and omniscience of God thus became
attributes of the man Jesus. In fact this may well be a
widespread notion among the simple faithful. Hence we
have reason to speak of monophysite tendencies which
affect many devout Christians even today. 'Monophysitism
is the temptation of pious but unthinking Christians.'[13]
When such a notion is carried to its logical conclusion
Christ is no longer seen as true man. His human appearance

[11] Ch. Möller, 'Jésus-Christ dans la mentalité moderne' in *Lumen Vitae*, VII, 1952,
pp. 549–67, p. 564 n. 1.

[12] Y. Congar, *Christ, Our Lady, and the Church*, London, 1957, p. 45.

[13] E. Masure, *Le sacrifice du chef*, 2nd ed., Paris, 1957, p. 115. Masure continues:
'The Christ whom they adore and to whom they pray is, as they say, the good God
(*le Bon Dieu*). By this they understand God who gives the impression, more or less,
of being a man, so as to be accessible to us. They do not deny him a body as did the
Docetists . . . But this body is only the historical garment of God now become
visible . . . The devotions upon which the Church does not keep a watchful enough
eye in the end easily slip into this unhealthy and tenuous heresy which, under a
Christian disguise, substitutes the simple theophanies of the Old Testament.' Cf.
Y. Congar, *op. cit.*, pp. 43 f.

is rather the visible shell of his divinity – not unlike the visible appearance of an angel. In the last analysis it is but the mysterious point at which God acts.

The religious interest that has spread abroad since the time of St Bernard and St Francis in the earthly life of Jesus has, for the most part, confined itself to those mysteries which are of decisive theological importance. These are the two motifs stressed in the Apostles' Creed and commemorated in the two great feasts of the Christian Year – Christmas and Easter. The motifs are the Incarnation with the related history of Jesus' infancy – the Christmas motif; and the work of redemption with the related history of the Passion and Resurrection – the Easter motif. Moreover, it is worth noting that it is more the visible side of the Easter motif that comes under review – the events concerning the Resurrection and the Ascension recorded in Holy Scripture, and regarded predominantly as events giving the final clue to the life of Jesus. Treated in this light and in many variants they become the subject of late medieval Christian art. They are no longer represented as decisive events in salvation-history, inaugurating the restoration of mankind, the new creation. This new creation had been the favourite theme of early Christian art, corresponding to the mind of the liturgy which, at Easter and throughout the octave of Easter, constantly keeps before our eyes the rising to new life of the redeemed, especially the newly baptized.

And so in the Middle Ages the faithful meditatively and reverently followed the tracks of our Lord's earthly life, revered his example, believed in the redemption his life contained; but when we come to the transition of the man Jesus into his new existence, and, even more, to the continuing life of the mediator and high-priest, the track is lost. He is simply the second person in the Godhead. People lose sight of the Christ of Easter, and, in the popular mind,

Christmas more and more takes the place of Easter as *the* Christian festival.[14] It is true that now Christ is represented in human form even within the Blessed Trinity, but so is the Father – as a venerable old man. This signifies, in all probability, that the human form is no longer taken really seriously; what is represented is not necessarily the human nature that was assumed at the Incarnation. Consequently from the tenth century onwards it became customary to represent all three divine persons in human form, sitting beside one another. Theology, and finally, at the beginning of modern times, ecclesiastical authority, objected to this form of representation, and also to the crude attempts at portraying the Trinity as a single human body (three-headed).[15] The trouble with such developments was that they obscured the mediatorial office of Christ. The humanity in which he stood at the head of our race, in which he rose as 'the first of them that slept' and preceded us into glory, in which he is the Head of his Church and we the members filled with his life, may well have been firmly attested as the object of faith in literature and in traditional formulae, but it has been pushed out to the fringe of consciousness.

This meant that for such a form of belief the gulf between man and God, bridged by Christ, opened up once more. On the one side is God, infinitely remote, on the other, man, a poor sinner, helpless before the justice of God. This is the actual feeling that we find in all its intensity in the greater part of the documents bearing witness to the devotional life of the early Middle Ages.[16] This is specially true of the

[14] It is significant that the attempt of the Reformers, too, to reinstate the feast of the Redemption, succeeded more with Good Friday than with Easter itself.

[15] Cf. K. Künstle, *Ikonographie der christlichen Kunst*, I, Freiburg, 1928, pp. 222 ff.

[16] To these belong the Irish *Book of Cerne* as well as the prayer-texts traditionally associated with the writings of Alcuin. Other texts have been published by A. Wilmart, *Auteurs spirituels et textes dévots du moyen-âge latin*, Paris, 1932. The decisive rôle of the Irish in this revolution has been clearly proved by W. Godel, o.s.b., in 'Irisches Beten im frühen Mittelalter' in *Zeitschrift für katholische Theologie*, LXXXV, 1963.

Apologies, those confessions of personal sinfulness, misery, and unworthiness, appearing since the seventh century even within the liturgy, and then slowly expanding until they reach unhealthy proportions, establishing themselves ultimately, like a creeping-plant, as private prayers of the priest, said at the altar. We see them taking root, in fact, in any nook or cranny left unfilled by the official prayer, even in the pauses supplied by the traditional singing of the *Gloria* and the *Sanctus* by the choir.[17] These apologies create the impression that people have never heard that we have been redeemed. In general they vanish in the eleventh century. The gentler approach to the sacrament of penance which became common at that time, and above all the new theological mood of emerging scholasticism, helped to brush them away.

Quite apart from such extreme phenomena, however, it is characteristic of the early medieval religious outlook that the mediatorial office of Christ, his closeness to men, which makes us his brothers and sisters, has receded in a striking fashion. A study of the letters of St Boniface proves that; 'The joyful awareness of being children of God does not control his attitude.'[18] The commands to lead a moral life are not based, as in St Paul, upon the facts of the life of Christ.[19] We must sketch a similar picture of the devotional life of Alcuin. His presentation of the doctrine of faith is no longer governed by salvation-history, but by the attempt to erect a system based upon the mystery of the Blessed Trinity. The faith he has 'received and learned' is closely merged with his religious thought wherein the consciousness of sin predominates and Christ is seen primarily as a severe judge.

[17] For details see Jungmann, *The Mass of the Roman Rite*, London, 1959, pp. 59 ff.
[18] E. Iserloh, 'Die Kontinuität des Christentums beim Übergang von der Antike zum Mittelalter' in *Trierer theol. Zeitschrift*, LXIII, 1954, pp. 193–205.
[19] *Ibid.*, pp. 203 f.

For Alcuin 'in Christ' has become changed to 'in front of Christ.'[20]

When the faithful almost lose sight of the glorified God-man, their image of the Church too is affected; for only in his glorified manhood can Christ be understood as Head of his Church. Only on this view can the Church be conceived as his mystical body.[21] As is well known, from the early Middle Ages until the twentieth century, the concept of the Church as the mystical body of Christ, while not altogether forgotten, was never very popular.[22] It did enjoy some importance for a while at the close of the Middle Ages, but in a degenerate form: the word was used as evidence of the secular power of the Pope, because the *corpus mysticum* could only have a single head.[23] The Pope therefore was installed as head of the mystical body. It was little wonder that the word progressively lost standing so that as recently as a few decades ago it could scarcely be found at all in dogmatic text-books. The fathers of the First Vatican Council showed little inclination to use it in a definition of the Church.[24]

The Church's hierarchical apparatus was stressed more and more. This happened as early as the period of Caroling-ian theology;[25] and so it remained until the catechisms of the nineteenth century. Even when the Church was being described as mother, people did not think, as formerly, of her sacramental function whereby she brought forth children in baptism, and fed them in the Eucharist, but of the hier-archical authority to direct, through which she disciplined

[20] H. B. Meyer, 'Alkuin zwischen Antike und Mittelalter' in *Zeitschrift für katholische Theologie*, LXXXI, 1959, pp. 306–50; 405–54;

[21] Cf. P. Michalon, 'Église corps mystique du Christ glorieux' in *Nouvelle Revue théolog.*, LXXIV, 1952, pp. 673–87.

[22] E. Mersch, *Le corps mystique du Christ*, II, Louvain, 1933, pp. 132, 139, 278 f.

[23] H. de Lubac, *Corpus mysticum*, Paris, 1944, pp. 131 ff.

[24] *Ibid.*, pp. 134 f.

[25] H. B. Meyer, *Alkuin*, pp. 427 ff.

her children.[26] And while the divine dignity of the ever-living Christ was being stressed and his human closeness to man suppressed, so too a new light came to be cast upon the Eucharist. No longer was it the daily bread of the children of God's family. Its reception became hedged about with more and more rules and restrictions, so that in the high Middle Ages the majority of the faithful scarcely dared exceed a single yearly communion.

All that was left to the pious soul was the distant contemplation of the Blessed Sacrament. About the turn of the twelfth century a unique eucharistic movement made itself felt: the sacred Host was to be displayed, not just immediately after the consecration, but frequently on other occasions also, so that it might be embraced with the eyes at least. In this way arose the forms of exposition of the Blessed Sacrament, and new forms of its veneration – the feast of Corpus Christi with its procession, the eucharistic blessing or Benediction, the monstrance and tabernacle, the Forty Hours' Prayer and Perpetual Adoration before the Blessed Sacrament. In some particular examples of Baroque architecture, the exposition throne would seem to have become more important than the table, which became overshadowed by the mighty superstructure. The reaction had already set in at the Council of Trent, but its full effect came to be felt only under Pope Pius X.

This attitude to the Eucharist in turn exerted an effect upon the conception of the church-building. We still frequently come upon the idea that it is only the presence of the Blessed Sacrament in the tabernacle which makes the physical building a house of God. Where there is no

[26] In an *Exultet* roll of the tenth century the words *mater Ecclesia* of the Easter *Exultet* were portrayed in the form of a woman sitting upon the church-building. In a related *Exultet* roll of the thirteenth century, the female figure has changed into a bishop. M. Avery, *The Exultet Rolls of South Italy*, Princeton, 1936, Plate CXL and Plate CLVIII.

tabernacle pious people often behave as though they were
in a secular building. This is a consequence of earlier ways
of thinking that has emerged only in modern times. At all
events the liturgy of the consecration of a church speaks of a
building without any tabernacle as a 'house of God and
gate of heaven.' Indeed the extravagant rite that had been
developed by the high Middle Ages cannot find imagery
and phrases enough to extol the dignity of the house into
which the relics of martyrs have entered, of which Christ has
taken possession, in which his faithful assemble, and
in which the holy sacrifice is offered. The reservation of
the Eucharist is never once mentioned. In this process
the one-sided emphasis on the real presence of Christ's
body has been allowed to overshadow many valuable
ideas.

From similar causes the popular understanding of Mass
and communion ultimately experienced modification. The
image in people's minds was no longer a reflexion of the
rising up of the grateful adoration of the Church in union
with her High Priest: the dominant thought was the descent
of God, the visitation of the Redeemer. This meant that
partial truths were becoming a substitute for the whole
truth.[27] (Since Isidore of Seville εὐχαριστία had come to be
translated *bona gratia*.) None can doubt that the adoration
of the Eucharist in many of its forms constitutes a permanent
enrichment of the Church's devotional life; but when, with
apparently rising awe, devotion concentrates only upon the
presence of God in the Eucharist, the danger arises that
the critical Christian, who is no longer attached to tradition,
may ask: 'Is God not present everywhere? Why do I have
to enter a church to meet God? Why, in particular, do I
require Mass and holy communion?' For this reason old

[27] Henry Fischer, *Eucharistiekatechese und liturgische Erneuerung*, Düsseldorf, 1959,
shows how catechesis still has to argue the point during the twentieth century.

Gustav Mey warned teachers of children against over-stressing the presence of God when giving instruction on the Blessed Sacrament, because by so doing the *mysterium* can so easily become a *monstrum*.[28]

In this way, in the mind of the average believer, the humanity of Christ, in virtue of which he is the fount of our salvation and our mediator with the Father, pales in the bright light of his divinity; and in consequence secondary mediators are forced into prominence. The beginnings of such developments are to be found at the close of Christian antiquity in the intense veneration of martyrs. The prolif-eration of legend was one symptom of this. Another was the desire to be buried beside martyrs so as to share in their assured resurrection. This desire was the cause, incidentally, of the destruction of so many frescoes in the catacombs.

In the early Middle Ages the development intensified; relics became the most precious treasure of every church; they were fetched from the most distant lands, and not always by irreproachable methods; the relics were placed in costly reliquaries which appeared under a thousand names and in a host of forms.[29] These reliquaries were the first things that people dared – from the ninth century onwards – to place upon the altar table, till then kept completely free from accessories. The veneration of saints, individually as well as in a company, became – in Alcuin's piety for example – a chief title to hope.[30] In the later Middle Ages the practice developed of taking particular saints as patrons of particular things or places or people. All of this added richness and colour to devotional life; but the thing which constituted the Christian's primary hope became somewhat obscured thereby. Even the official Church had

[28] Gustav Mey, *Vollständige Katechesen*[4], Freiburg, 1879, p. 364.
[29] Cf. J. Braun, *Die Reliquiare*, Freiburg, 1940. Cf. also a survey in the *Lexikon für Theologie und Kirche*, VIII, 1936, pp. 805 ff.
[30] H. B. Meyer, *Alkuin*, p. 448.

incorporated the veneration of saints in the intercessions of public worship at an early date, but in such a way that it was subordinated to the over-all plan: the Church addressed her prayer to God *intercedentibus sanctis martyribus* – but this *intercessio* was certainly to some extent only an intensified sounding-board of our true title to hope. The collect ended as always – *per Christum Dominum nostrum*.

In the past few centuries another factor has influenced the preaching of the faith along the same lines, enriching it, but also tending to destroy it. This factor is theological science. Necessary as its function is within the Church, especially in a period of intense spiritual life, important as it is for theological science to establish the harmony between reason and faith, through its speculative penetration of the facts of revelation, thus preventing the world of faith from sinking into a sphere of unreality, it can accomplish this only by way of progressive analysis, through ever new distinctions and concepts which in themselves lead further and further away from the central facts of the order of salvation. A flourishing theology is the Church's pride. At the same time it constitutes a temptation for the preaching of the faith to want to offer as many as possible of her treasures to the faithful in general, thus overburdening the kerygma with things of second and third rank. It is the temptation to go beyond the principle that dogma as such is not kerygma but merely the 'norm of the kerygma.'[31] It surprises us a little today when we observe that in the hymn *Lauda Sion* the doctrine of substance and accident as well as that about the whole and the smallest fragment of the Eucharistic species are fully worked out. In modern catechisms, among other things, a whole self-contained section has been developed on grace and the means of grace, and this regularly appears as a kind of appendix to moral teaching, quite separated from the

---

[31] J. Ratzinger, *Christozentrik in der Verkündigung*, p. 10.

exposition of the facts of salvation-history. In such a system concepts appear that were still unknown even to the theologians of the thirteenth century: supernatural endowment; sanctifying grace; infused virtues; revival of merit. The effects of the individual sacraments were enumerated in a series of points – often a lengthy series – and each time the increase of sanctifying grace was the concept specially stressed – except with respect to the sacraments of the dead.

The sermons of the declining Middle Ages, too, often made a rather unfortunate use of scholastic science. Their doctrinaire attitude and broad treatment of theological controversies and scholastic subtleties were already being attacked by Erasmus and other humanists. Catechesis was too imperfectly developed for any great damage to result in that field. On the whole people were satisfied with traditional formulae and recitations. The confession-booklets of the period, however, show that in the field of moral teaching there was widespread use of distinctions, definitions, and casuistic problems, useful no doubt to the confessor, but calculated rather to divert the Christian's eye from more important things, although supposed to aid him in his Christian life. Even the recitations we have mentioned, which summarized points of biblical and theological doctrine, virtues, and sins, were for ever being multiplied, especially in the form of septenaries and other often trivial sequences, so that there too we discover that a basic formula such as the Apostles' Creed could be ousted or overshadowed by others that were set in the same series with it.

As we know, the Reformation storm was aimed not least at this proliferation of peripheral things in the Church's teaching of the faith and in Church life. The tragedy was that justified criticism – soon to be indulged in by perceptive Catholics too – forthwith became involved in the denial of essential articles of faith. The Council of Trent corrected many blatant abuses in Church life. For the rest its work was mainly the defence of the traditional substance of the faith, the clarification of all that was genuine Catholic tradition in the practice of the sacraments, the sacrifice of the Mass, the veneration of saints, and indulgences. The totality of these rulings on faith could not produce a harmonious, self-contained summary of the Christian revelation, but merely an assuring of all the threatened points, to which attention was now directed with increased concentration. The Council of Trent, however, did feel the need for a harmonious, complete summary of the faith, and at the twenty-fifth session commissioned the compilation of such a book. This was published in 1566 as the *Catechismus Romanus,* a work which represented a great advance, especially in its over-all structure. In it the host of secondary formulae are suppressed, the Creed assumes its rightful, dominant place, the doctrine of the sacraments follows the exposition of the Creed as the expansion of the doctrine of the faith. Many individual topics, too, are once again integrated organically into the total picture, as when the phrase *communio sanctorum* is understood as a development of the concept of the Church.

In general, however, in the age following the Council, the attitudes of the declining Middle Ages to preaching and teaching and to the devotional life were maintained in so far as they were theologically unobjectionable. Indeed in so far as they were attacked by innovators they became even more entrenched. This is particularly true of the emphasis upon the real presence in the Eucharist and in the corresponding cult of the Blessed Sacrament. It is equally apparent with respect to the cult of the saints and of relics. In the Baroque period once again the Church became filled with the relics of alleged saints of the catacombs. But now it was the veneration of the mother of God that pressed more and more into the foreground, and with it, more or less consciously, one of the central mysteries of the order of salvation – the Incarnation. From the sixteenth century onwards Marian shrines and Marian pilgrimages arose in many places. On other points doctrine was now sharpened as antithesis to heretical denial; in the concept of faith, assent was emphasized so that in many catechisms it became the regulative word in the definition of faith. Authority in the Church was pushed into the forefront. The faithful became used to seeing the Church in her official ministers who looked after them and led them. The *opus operatum* was the aspect of the doctrine and practice of the sacraments that was stressed: the valid performance of the sacramental rite was the all-important thing. Correspondingly there arose the temptation to view the liturgical forms, now the exclusive concern of the clergy, one-sidedly from the rubrical angle, and to undervalue the personal, subjective participation in sacrament and liturgy by the faithful. Genuine religious life had, therefore, to propagate itself chiefly through acclimatization to a fixed environment with its approved order. Ultimately, everything necessary for salvation was contained within this order.

Clear-sighted men had already raised objections to the doubtful aspects of the traditional *status quo*. Muratori, for example, complained of the extravagances in the cult of relics and of saints.[32] Rosmini complained that one of the five wounds of the Church was the estrangement of the Christian people from the liturgy of the Church.[33] More

---

[32] Cf. Muratori, *De ingeniorum moderatione in religionis negotio*, Parma, 1714; *idem*, *De la regolata devozione de'cristiani*, 1747. This second work was violently attacked in several replies, because it dared to object to accretions in the cult of our Lady also; but after examination it was declared irreproachable by Pope Benedict XIV. C. Castiglioni, 'L. A. Muratori e la pietà cristiana' in *Scuola cattolica*, LXIV, 1936, pp. 24–34.

[33] A. Rosmini, *Delle cinque piaghe della santa Chiesa,* Brussels, 1848, pp. 9–25.

important, however, was the fact that through God's providence positive forces had also been set in motion which set about leading religious thought and life away from its fragmentation and disintegration back along definite lines. Among these forces we count the *Spiritual Exercises* of St Ignatius, with their conducting of the soul to the service of God in imitation of Christ, and the popular missions that these *Exercises* inspired and which reached a wide circle of people. Of special importance is the powerful impulse towards devotion to the Sacred Heart of Jesus, a devotion which for many provided once more a central idea amidst the confusion of devotional life. All searching and groping could now cease with the assurance that in Christ God's love had really come to man.

On the other hand, the past few centuries have seen fresh powers of dissolution at work. First of all there was the cultural surge of the Enlightenment. The effect of this movement could not exactly be described as a further disintegration of the substance of the faith. On the contrary the movement sought with uncanny logic to disseminate a simple Christianity, freed from all accretions. But now the whole of Christian doctrine was threatened with dissolution and decay, because little now was preserved of revelation and dogma except the empty words. The substance of faith was replaced by a philosophy of life based upon reason and virtue.

In the process, not only was God made to appear very remote, the one who set the whole structure of the world in motion at the beginning, and then left it to the ruling powers of nature, and to man; but Christianity too was represented as a religious system, founded by Christ, it is true, but thereafter handed over to human management.[34] Although

---

[34] Cf. F. X. Arnold, *Grundsätzliches und Geschictliches zur Theologie der Seelsorge*, Freiburg, 1949, pp. 75 ff.

such views were not widely held within the Church in quite such an undisguised form, the notion that Christ had merely founded the Church and endowed it with its necessary organization tended towards that isolating way of speaking of the authority and sacraments of the Church which paid little heed any longer to their supra-temporal root in Christ, and, on the other hand, saw in Christ's redemptive passion little more than a model of heroic virtue. Moreover, all this was bound to strengthen the tendency to regard Christ's appearance in this world merely as a process which has been concluded with his death, and to neglect the continuing activity of the Lord who had entered, through death, into glorified life, so that devout contemplation merely held before the mind the *Christus patiens* who once was, instead of gazing up primarily to *Christus passus et semper vivens*.[35]

By the middle of the nineteenth century the Enlightenment had spent itself as a force within the leadership and pastoral outlook of the Church. Not until the present day has naturalistic thinking in the spirit of the Enlightenment become a serious temptation for the great mass of Catholics, as a result of the expansion of the picture of the universe, the triumph of the natural sciences, and the opening up of undreamed of secular possibilities. In addition, international traffic and communications have introduced all peoples, all religions, all philosophies of life to each other. Everything threatens to become relative. A blurred Christianity that is no longer aware of its own power now faces a double threat.

What has been said is not meant to be an indictment of the proclamation of the faith in the earlier periods of the Church's life. This earlier proclamation had the good fortune to take place very largely within a Christian environ-

[35] Cf. F. X. Arnold, *Seelsorge aus der Mitte der Heilsgeschichte*, Freiburg, 1956, pp. 51 ff.

ment. In these circumstances it was sufficient to transmit the required knowledge of the faith without falsification, even in conditions of far-reaching disintegration. Today, in a secularized society, this is not enough. When preaching the faith we must try once again to regain the total, consolidated power of the Christian message.

V

Addition or Concentration?

IT IS significant that many of the experts in prayer, and
many masters of the spiritual life, who have emerged
especially in the later phases of Church history, and who
have gathered a group of disciples around them, have seen
the substance of faith in a definite, personal perspective.
Very often, indeed, some favourite idea has dominated
their religious aspiration.

St Frances of Rome (d. 1440), for example, was pre-
occupied with the notion of the guardian angels; St Louis
Grignion de Montfort (d. 1717) considered himself the
slave of the mother of God; for St Caspar Bufalo (d. 1837)
the Precious Blood was the centre and sum of all piety; for
St Pierre Julien Eymard (d. 1868) it was the triumph of the
Blessed Sacrament (*le beau règne de Jésus-hostie*). Frequently it
was some mystical experience that determined where the
accent came to be placed. There are many ways along which
God's grace can come to men. The stars of heaven can be
viewed through a very small chink. In the end the decisive
thing is the completeness of the self-abandonment with
which a man yields himself to God's grace, no matter what
name he gives to that response. It is true that very often
the followers of these great ones have been left holding
only the husk of that fervent prayer. Their temptation has
been to make a pot-pourri with the dried blooms of a
summer long past. These flowers are most precious and
beautiful; but are they still alive?

We are confronted with the phenomenon of the con-
servation and augmentation of forms of devotion and
meditation. We need not be surprised to find in some votive-

chapel at the edge of a village not only the appropriate original image of, it may be, the Mother of Sorrows, but also a whole collection of others – Sacred Heart statues, stucco figures of St Antony or of St Teresa of Lisieux, three or four more pictures of our Lady, several votive plaques of the Blessed Trinity, all in the tawdry style of the nineteenth century. Very often what we find in the prayer-books of the last century – even of this century – is not so very different. These contain prayers, not just for all occasions – as they should – but also from the most diverse sources. The morning prayer, for example, is not content with thanksgiving, and praise of God, and a petition as in the collect at Prime, '. . . that we may not fall into any sin, and that all our thoughts, words, and deeds may be directed to the fulfilling of thy will'; but there have to be prayers to the separate persons of the Trinity, to the guardian angel, to Mary, and St Joseph;[1] there have to be acts of faith, hope, and love, as well as the 'good intention' contained in the morning offering; then one has to associate oneself with every Mass that is being offered the whole world over, and to express the intention of gaining every indulgence it is possible to gain.

The same sort of accumulation is frequently seen in religious organizations which threaten to become a conglomeration. There can be no doubt that there was a genuine and serious pastoral concern behind the founding of the apostolate for men in 1910. The task of this apostolate has been described thus: 'to win men to the practice of monthly communion through devotion to the Sacred Heart.' Apostolic work was expected to flow from this.

---

[1] Fr. J. Peters (d. 1957), a dogmatic theologian of high repute, in his book *Einkehr. Anregungen zur Pflege priesterlichen Geistes*, Bonn, 1950, pp. 18 ff., demands that at his morning devotions the priest, in addition to Mass, Breviary, and meditation, pray to God the Father, the Son, the Holy Spirit, the mother of God, his angel guardian, and to other individual saints.

The aim was to make apostles – an ideal in harmony with
the times. To encourage men to receive communion every
month is a fine aim, provided it is not supposed to occur
in an extra-liturgical form. The Sacred Heart devotion, too,
was a tried and tested method of deepening religious life.
But was the permanent adding together of these three
religious aims a sound measure, especially under the title
of an apostolate which, in our period of Catholic Action,
requires for its interior edification a few more explicit
preconditions besides regular monthly communion?[2] We
might ask also if it is essential in the apostolate of prayer to
link with devotion to the Sacred Heart the notion of the
mediation of the Immaculate Heart of Mary. The practice
of consecration, too, which since the seventeenth century
has developed into an independent practice out of the
dedication of sodalities on their reception into the Marian
congregation,[3] can lead to unnatural multiplication, all
the more noticeable since the act of consecration implies
singularity, for consecration is essentially the total surrender
of one's own self, an act which, in the true sense, can be
performed only to God himself. Acts of consecration are
recommended to Christ the Lord, to the Sacred Heart, to
the Heart of Jesus present in the Eucharist, to the Holy
Spirit, to Mary, to the Immaculate Heart of Mary, to the
Holy Family.[4] Every one of these acts of consecration has a
rational foundation, and, moreover, ecclesiastical approval.[5]
Ultimately, however, every Catholic Christian ought to
realize that his consecration lies primarily in his baptism,

[2] On the adaptation of the men's apostolate in Germany since 1945, cf. H. Ostermann, 'Mannerwerk' in *Lexikon für Theologie und Kirche*, VI, 1961, p. 1363.

[3] See Jungmann, *Pastoral Liturgy*, London, 1962, pp. 295–314, 'From Patrocinium
to the Act of Consecration.'

[4] We can see how such acts of consecration are in danger of becoming empty
forms, if we read the report of how a certain American bishop consecrated every
individual and all families to the Sacred Heart of Jesus through television on the
feast of the Immaculate Conception in 1959.

[5] See *Enchiridion Indulgentiarum*, Rome, 1950, Index, s.v. *consecratio*.

and that it is strengthened and corroborated by every serious participation in the sacramental sacrifice of the New Testament. In the end even the ecclesiastical approbation of religious practices and devotions, even its endowment of them with indulgences, beneficial as both of these things are, cannot be the norm for the real building up of religious life; for these devotions are concerned always, or almost always, with particularities, with devotion in certain specific circumstances – that is with separate stones in the building. A collection of even the very best stones still does not produce a building people can live in.

It is conceivable that such conglomeration in the devotional life of the simple Christian, whose one idea is to save his soul, will often assume fantastic forms. He holds fast to all that the Church teaches, fulfils all his Christian duties, frequents Mass and communion, and then looks around anxiously to see if there are any further means of assurance. He takes up every fresh devotion, joins several fraternities, wears the scapulars of various orders, tries to gain every available indulgence, keeps his eyes open for any new visions and revelations, travels long journeys to glean a scrap of advice from the lips of some mystically endowed young woman, and all the while lives in a state of worry over the salvation of his soul. The inevitable consequence of this sort of thing is that all sense of proportion and all feeling for religious rhythm are utterly lost.[6]

We do not mean to condemn or misjudge the zeal of those who in their devotions or in their direction of souls make use of these by-ways in the devotional life, provided they do stick to approved forms [7] On the contrary, with Karl

[6] For example, some time ago the author received a parcel bearing a sticker containing the words: 'Repeat frequently: "Blessed be the immaculate Heart of Mary." Also ask your friends to do likewise.'

[7] Ecclesiastical authority only warns us against extreme cases, as for example against the modern devotion to the divine mercy: cf. *A.A.S.,* LI, 1959, p. 271.

Rahner we are happy to extol 'even the little gate of a private revelation,' but again with him we would add: 'Even the best devotion which we all ought to practise is still not the whole of Christianity,'[8] nor is the sum of all devotions, especially when these have emerged from formless accumulation. Indeed the classic form of Christian piety lies nearer to that style which places the accent in religious life not at the centre, but upon an essential point in the Christian faith. Since the late Middle Ages in hagiographical literature we are constantly reading of saints who had a special devotion to our Lady.[9] In the Baroque period it was already a rule of the perfect Christian life that it should be renowned for its special devotion to Mary and the Blessed Sacrament.[10] It is obvious that such affirmations are possible only at a stage when the world of the Christian faith has lost its unified completeness in the popular mind, and the process of disintegration is already well advanced, so that accretion and eclecticism are bound to result.

We point out these things now solely with the intention of bringing out more clearly the specific issue with which this pastoral-theological study is concerned, and not in order to unsettle anyone who, through these or similar forms of devotion, has attained a genuine religious life. In the devotional life, too, God is able to write straight along crooked lines. But what works with an individual need not always work as a pastoral prescription, still less as a pastoral programme for our time.

It is not summation but concentration that must be today's solution, a concentration that rejects nothing of

[8] Karl Rahner, *Visionen und Prophezeihungen*, Freiburg, 1958, p. 84.

[9] The Roman Breviary makes this claim for St Raymond of Peñafort (d. 1275) and St Bridget (d. 1373). The Benedictine order regards Ambrosius Autpertus (d. 784) as one of the first to venerate our Lady. J. Leclercq, 'Dévotion et théologie mariales dans le monachisme bénédictin' in *Maria*, II, Paris, 1952, pp. 547–78, esp. p. 551.

[10] Jungmann, *Pastoral Liturgy*, London, 1962, p. 86.

value, but puts it in its proper place. Pastoral care that is
intent upon essentials will keep many roads open, but all
roads will converge upon the one true road of salvation.
In the end we shall find that the worship of the Church not
only points us to this one road of salvation, but also shows
us the pattern of true concentration: the Litany of the
Saints contains almost the whole of Church history, and all
the needs of suffering mankind find expression therein, but
everything is set within the framework of a mighty,
ordered scheme, and at the end is gathered together in the
great stream of the Church's collects. In the liturgical year,
too, a host of secondary devotional forms are indicated:
there we find not only numerous saints, each one of whom
God has sought out in a different way, but also much about
the various ways they have followed and tested. Here we
find the Holy Name or the Sacred Heart of Jesus being
venerated, there Corpus Christi and the Precious Blood,
there the Rosary or the commemoration of the holy souls;
but all of these are merely the overtones and undertones:
they do not change the melody, they do not deflect the
prayer of the Church from its main stream, rather, they
deepen and enrich the mighty sound of that voice of
adoration which rises unceasingly to God *per ipsum et cum
ipso et in ipso*.

VI

The Kerygma

As ALREADY hinted, what we are primarily concerned with is the renewal of the kerygma. In catechesis and sermon, in the shape of public worship and of the place of worship, and, as far as possible, in every expression of Church life, Christian doctrine ought to be led back to its original, unified power, so that above all else it is the kerygma itself that is heard.

What do we mean by the kerygma?[1] Kerygma is a biblical concept meaning 'that which is preached.' It denotes, therefore, the content of preaching, that is what Christ himself proclaimed and what his apostles proclaimed abroad as his heralds: that the kingdom of God had entered the world, thus disclosing salvation to mankind. It denotes the original preaching,[2] at first addressed to those who did not yet believe,[3] but which was also intended to provide the core and basis of all subsequent guidance and instruction of believing Christians, and which ought to

[1] Clarification would not seem to be superfluous. The word is indeed often used in a very loose sense to denote a compendium of catechesis and sermon (Hemlein), a vital or picturesque presentation (de Coninck, Fabro), or pastoral theology in general. A short and apposite discussion of the meaning of kerygmatic efforts is given by M. Ramsauer, 'Analysis of the kerygmatic approach' in *Mission Bulletin*, II, 1959, pp. 351–60 (separate pamphlet Hongkong, 1961). A systematic treatment is given by J. Hofinger, *The Art of Teaching Christian doctrine*[2], Notre Dame, Indiana, 1962.

[2] H. Schürmann, 'Kerygma' in *Lexikon für Theologie und Kirche*, v, 1961, pp. 122–5.

[3] A. Rétif, 'Qu'est-ce que le kérygme?' in *Nouvelle Revue théol.*, LXXI, 1949, pp. 910–22; idem., *Foi au Christ et Mission d'après les Actes des Apôtres*, Paris, 1953, pp. 14 ff. Rétif distinguishes κήρυγμα from subsequent instruction in the διδαχή (catechesis) and finally in the διδασκαλία. For a more detailed explanation of the terminology cf. D. Grasso, 'Evangelizzazione, Catechesi, Omilia' in *Gregorianum*, XLII, 1961, pp. 242–67. Grasso points out that French authors are inclined to join with the exegetes and to restrict the concept of kerygma to mean the initial preaching, with regard to the task in dechristianized regions (pp. 251 f.).

become all the more clearly sounded in those places where the paths of faith have become overgrown, and where a fresh need has arisen for orientation and sign-posting.[4] The kerygma is the announcement of facts, above all of the facts through which God himself has intervened in human history and uttered his call to mankind. Thus it is more than just a doctrine, first of all, because it is not concerned with the clarification of concepts and principles, but chiefly with the account of happenings, and secondly, because it has to do with something that man cannot be allowed to grasp with his mind alone: it concerns God's call and invitation. For this reason the sermons of the apostles were testimonies, attestation of those things they had 'seen and heard' (I Jn 1. 1; Acts 4. 20), that Christ had died for us and risen from the dead, and that by reason of this fact all nations were now to have preached to them repentance and the forgiveness of sins (Luke 24. 47).

The demand that the kerygma ought to be accentuated in all our preaching is now directed not simply against the sheer addition of ever new details of knowledge and forms of devotion, but also against all excessive splitting up of the substance of faith within preaching, and against all rank growth around the fringe. At least in our day, it stands in a certain tension towards dogmatic theology as this has traditionally come to be transmitted in theological instruction. At all events it is striking that, since this demand was formulated,[5] lively discussion has arisen about this very tension, and about this alone, about the question, that is,

[4] This is almost universally the case, and hence the kerygma must form the norm of preaching, as D. Grasso emphasizes in 'Il kerygma e la predicatione' in *Gregorianum*, XLI, 1960, pp. 424–50. Rétif, *Foi au Christ*, p. 11, also stresses that kerygma remains a timeless aspect of the Christian message. Similarly cf. I. Hermann, 'Kerygma und Kirche' in *Neutestamentliche Aufsätze*, Festschrift J. Schmidt, Regensburg, 1963, pp. 110–14.

[5] J. A. Jungmann, *Die Frohbotschaft und unsere Glaubersverkündigung*, Regensburg, 1936, pp. 25 ff.

whether the demands, associated with the kerygma, for greater closeness to life, for emphasis upon the message of salvation, for Christocentricity, necessitate the construction of an autonomous theology alongside traditional scholastic theology.[6] This necessity has been denied – with good reason. The happy outcome of discussion has been the conviction that all of these demands can and ought to be fulfilled by dogmatic theology rightly understood, and that we must resist the temptation to turn theology into a supernatural metaphysic and to treat of the actualities of salvation-history only in passing – under pressure from a Platonic–Aristotelian concept of science which recognizes only the universal and not the historically unique as the subject-matter of science. In the end the true task of Christian theology remains as it was – to use the means at its disposal to illumine and explain the order of the world established by the fact of Christ. It is true that it need not stand still beside the historical fact (nor need preaching); certainly it is concerned with the timeless significance of this fact. Christ's resurrection is no mere past event, but continues in the activity of the Church and in the life of grace of the faithful throughout all ages. And so St Paul can point the Greeks, who seek wisdom, to Christ crucified (I Cor. I. 22) in whom the wisdom and power of God are given to us. Hence theology, too, if it places Christ at its centre and never loses sight of him, need lose none of its breadth of horizon.[7] It remains the honourable right and duty of

[6] At last we have a comprehensive review of this whole discussion by A. A. Estebán Romero, 'La controversia en torno a la teologia kerigmatica' in XV. *Semana española de Teologia*, Madrid, 1956, pp. 367–409. This work contains a thorough bibliography. Jungmann indicates the main points under discussion in his *Katechetik²*, Vienna, 1955, pp. 309–15. These problems are dealt with in a wider setting by C. Colombo, 'La metodologia e la sistemazione teologica' in *Problemi e orientamenti di Teologia dommatica*, I, Milan, 1957, pp. 1–56. Karl Rahner sums up in 'Kerygmatische Theologie' in *Lexikon für Theologie und Kirche*, VI, 1961, p. 126.

[7] These ideas have been specially elaborated by G. Corti, 'Alla radice della controversia kerigmatica' in *Scuola Cattolica*, LXXVIII, 1950, pp. 283–301.

the science of faith to examine all questions that are or can
be addressed to revelation as it encounters critical reason,
whether in the form of heretical tendencies or of fresh
probings of the human spirit into the mysteries of God,
provided only that the sense of the 'bright darkness of the
mystery' is preserved even by theology. We can continue
to be grateful for all the findings of dogmatic theology,
even those that have a rather accidental character.[8] But
amidst all the complexities of distinctions, theses, and
hypotheses, the *leitmotiv* of salvation-history must be
preserved. The 'kerygmatic climaxes' must once more
come into their own.[9]

The extent to which theology can accommodate itself to
preaching will depend in the end upon whether it regards
God in himself (*Deus sub ratione Deitatis*) as its proper subject-matter and the central object of all its efforts – and this
is implied by the name 'theo-logia' that has been used since
the hey-day of scholasticism – or takes as its subject-matter
God in so far as he has condescended to us in Christ; it
depends, that is, upon whether or not theology is always to
some extent self-limited by the way of salvation and the
outlook from man's angle.[10] The pre-scholastic beginnings
of theology certainly kept to the latter prescription; for
them, theology was the theology of redemption;[11] and

[8] Cf. Hugo Rahner, *Eine Theologie der Verkündigung*, 2nd ed., Freiburg, 1939, p.
8. Rahner affirms that the development of theology 'never proceeds from the
organism of the tenacity of purpose that is at the heart of dogmas, but is independent
of the contingencies of the contesting of dogmas that arises from without, and at
the same time independent of the genius of great theologians.'

[9] Fr. Hofmann, *Theologie und Glaube*, XLVIII, 1956, p. 306.

[10] Cf. P. Hitz, 'Théologie et catéchèse' in *Nouvelle Revue théol.*, LXXVII, 1955, pp.
897–923: " The central point of our *theologia viatorum* as of our Christian faith is not
'God in himself', but 'the glory of God in the face of Christ' (2 Cor. 4. 6)." p. 915.

[11] G. Fittkau, *Der Begriff des Mysteriums bei Johannes Chrysostomus*, Bonn, 1953,
p. 213, says: 'As for his apostolic master (St Paul) so for Chrysostom the whole of
theology is soteriology.' Very often θεολογία was used to denote the doctrine of
God himself, and οίκονομία to denote the scheme of redemption. Hugh of St
Victor (d. 1141) was still abiding by the historical-biblical principle. The compendium of revelation in his work *De sacramentis* treats, in Book I, of the period

today also there are prominent theologians who adopt a similar view of their task.[12]

If then dogmatic theology and pastoral teaching once again draw closer together and a special theology of teaching and preaching becomes unnecessary, nevertheless preaching itself can never become simply identical with theology. Theology must always remain scientific, analytical, in search of knowledge, a builder of systems, and to that extent a self-contained study of the contents of revelation, whereas preaching has to transmit the content of revelation thus illumined in all its unity and power as a doctrine of redemption and a guide for man along his road – a task which certainly will have to be performed with greater or less use of theological knowledge, according to the state of education of those who hear, but which can never simply coincide with theological science. Kerygma and dogma are never simply identical. In recent centuries this fact has frequently been overlooked. We have already referred to signs of this in the history of the catechisms.[13]

---

from the creation of the world to the Incarnation, in Book II, of the period from the Incarnation until the consummation of the world. By contrast Abelard and Peter the Lombard favour a more rationalist systematization. H. Cloes, 'La systématisation théologique pendant la première moitié du XIIe siècle' in *Ephem. Theol. Lovanienses*, XXXIV, 1958, pp. 277–329. Cloes recommends contemporary theologians to follow the way of the Victorine master (p. 328).

[12] Cf. M. Schmaus, *Katholische Dogmatik*, 6th ed., Munich, 1960, p. 31. The chief subject-matter of theology is God – 'in so far as he has revealed himself to us in Christ.' Hence in every statement 'reference to Christ and to the kingdom of God revealed in him must shine through' (p. 33). J. Ratzinger, 'Christozentrik in der Verkündigung' in *Trierer theol. Zeitschrift*, 1961, p. 2, describes the ontological statements of Christology as 'assurances of the true confession of Christ' which are 'theologically necessary but not the primary subject-matter of preaching.' According to Karl Rahner, *Theological Investigations*, I, London, and Baltimore, 1961, pp. 19–37, special dogmatics contains only two sections – once the preliminary problems of 'Formal and Fundamental Theology' have been settled: 'Man (and his world) (including Christology)' and the 'Fall and the Redemption.' Even the doctrine of the Blessed Trinity falls within this plan. Cf. also his observation that in principle it would be possible 'to interpret all theological propositions in the whole of dogmatics as propositions of theological anthropology,' *Lexikon für Theologie und Kirche*, I, 1957, p. 624.

[13] Cf. above, p. 46 f.

Even today it is not superfluous to point this out. I have before me an issue of a journal published by a group of Catholic university youths in Vienna in 1959. This publication contained a series of articles by a theological correspondent. The title of the series was 'The Church grants an audience' and this was the problem under discussion: 'Are those who find themselves in possession of sanctifying grace, the infused virtues, and the gifts of the Holy Spirit, also dependent upon the action of intermittent, actual graces?' Is this sort of excerpt from theological textbooks not offering stones instead of bread? In addition I can turn to the fly-leaf in which an American catechist recommends his brochure *Supernatural Life* – which has enjoyed two editions since 1955 – describing it as a 'little book about the sixteen gifts of the soul in a state of grace.' He arrives at this number by the artless adding up of sanctifying grace, the three theological virtues, the four cardinal virtues, divine indwelling, and the seven gifts of the Holy Spirit – all of which gifts are separately discussed as an introduction for the catechesis of children.[14] Surely such a procedure is but the meaningless stringing together of theological concepts under the semblance of thoroughness. In both cases mentioned an inappropriate use is made of theological science in preaching. The preaching of the faith is not popularized theology.

For the perfecting of the Christian life, and also for a more detailed knowledge of its conditions, theological analysis of the supernatural life – quite apart from large-scale enumerations – is of very doubtful value. It cannot be important, for example, to draw an explicit contrast between the infused virtues (almost certainly misunderstood under this name) and sanctifying grace (which one would

---

[14] Because my name has been strikingly misused on the fly-leaf I must mention the pamphlet: *Supernatural Life*, 2nd edition, 1955, by Paul M. Baier.

seem to *possess* as though it were some material thing); still less ought one to impute theologumena concerning habitual and actual grace to the laity, when these things are of merely peripheral interest even to theologians.

In teaching the faith we must indeed distinguish between doctrines and concepts that are given in revelation as enlightenment and direction, and those which are deduced and affirmed in the vast speculative ramifications of a theological system in order to harmonize data or to consolidate the position in face of opposition.[15] Often the front line of defence has to be set up far away from the fruitful fields of the message of salvation. Even the Church's pronouncements on doctrine, almost always aimed against errors in human thinking, are intended primarily as but negative delimitations of the doctrinal heritage. Anyone who tries to elaborate the doctrine of the Church solely from the definitions he can collect in Denzinger might perhaps compose a picture of the ecclesiastical hierarchy, but scarcely an appropriate over-all picture of the Church. Consequently it is not out of place to utter a warning: catechesis as the exercise of the official teaching office in the Church must be on its guard against regarding, in an unbalanced fashion, the most recently defined or precisely formulated dogmas as the most important.[16]

---

[15] Ratzinger, *op. cit.*, p. 10: 'Dogma marks out the boundaries of preaching.'
[16] Cf. P. A. Liégé, 'Contenu et pédagogie da la prédication chrétienne' in *Maison Dieu*, XXXIX, 1954, pp. 23–7, 35.

C

VII

Christocentricity

AT ALL times the preaching of the faith must be orientated towards the kerygma; and Christocentricity is essential to the kerygma. Christocentricity is not, however, a geometrical concept. By it we do not mean that the figure of our Lord must literally be at the centre of every exposition, or that his name must be expressly mentioned at every turn. What we do mean is that in every separate point of doctrine the objectively existing reference to the person of Christ should always shine through the exposition, thus drawing it together to form a unity, a living cosmos. The law of the Old Testament was a school-master to bring men to Christ. In Christ God's redemptive purpose for man has taken shape. The Church is the assembly of those who belong to him. In the sacraments it is he who acts and sanctifies us. Grace is a sharing in his closeness to God, in his divine Sonship. To live a Christian life is to live in Christ. The kingdom of God will be consummated when he returns.

This style of exposition has great advantages, quite apart from its unity and the self-containment of the total picture it provides. The doctrinal edifice loses its coldness and stiffness and becomes a living organism. At the centre there stands a person, the noblest, the greatest, the one in whom the love of God has appeared within the world of men, or, as modern French authors like to reiterate: Christianity is not something to which one has to give assent, but someone whom we meet. In this way Christianity appears no longer as an aggregate of duties and services which we men have to perform, but is primarily the work of God who has graciously come down to meet us in Christ. In this form it truly appears as good news which comes to us from God. Through the new creation which is thus established we see ourselves taken into a vast objective order. Hidden in Christ, we become raised above all individualistic constriction and all anxieties. In him God has chosen us for eternal life. Finally, such a manner of presentation brings with it the additional benefit that the reference to Christ on each occasion expresses the basis of our faith, thus making us aware that faith is not demanded arbitrarily. It becomes plain that the Church's sole desire is to bring those who belong to her close to Christ, and that in the end it is he who speaks through the Church, he who demands the obedience of faith. No one is exempted from faith, nor should be; but to some extent it is demanded only once for all and only with respect to its distinct title.

It is true, however, that such a manner of speaking has its own dangers. What we say about Christ may become a mere phrase; we may extol Christ as Lord and King and God, citing every passage in Scripture and tradition which tells of his greatness, and yet may miss their true meaning, because we simply interchange the words 'God' and 'Christ,' thus upsetting once again the whole structure of the world of faith. Despite every good intention, such a manner of speaking would lapse into that monophysitism to which we have already referred.[1] Our picture of Christ would have succumbed to a 'false divinizing tendency.' 'In Christ, God is not primarily concerned to intervene in human history in terms of his divinity. This is not the purpose of the Incarnation. His primary purpose is to be in the world and act in the world as a man.'[2]

[1] Cf. above, p. 38 f.
[2] A. Grillmeier, 'Zum Christusbild der heutigen katholischen Theologie' in *Fragen der Theologie heute*, Einsiedeln, 1957, p. 285.

Undoubtedly there is a theologically acceptable mode of speech which emphasizes the divine greatness of Christ. This is the language which became more and more prominent in the Eastern Church in its reaction against Arianism. Here we find, as the typical predication about our Lord: 'Christ our God.' This is the language which goes back to Alexandrian theology, and which established itself after the Council of Chalcedon in the Byzantine sphere, especially within the Byzantine liturgy.[3] Behind this lies the view that in the Incarnation the Logos assumed and divinized human nature, and that this divinization reached its final and perfect development in the Resurrection, and became the source of redemption for the whole of mankind.[4] This view affirms the two natures in Christ without minimizing either; it does not place them simply side by side; but, while preserving the Chalcedonian insistence on 'unconfused yet unseparated', it none the less stresses the divine nature of the Logos as the predicate-subject, and in so doing can appeal to beginnings that are present in the Gospel of St John. But even if this does not deny the redemptive significance of our Lord's human nature and of his earthly life, which sanctifies all human life, this is only one side of the movement of salvation-history – the movement from above downwards, the coming down of redemption from God to men, the passive reception. This is the side which on this view comes into the light, whereas the responsive movement from below upwards, in which the man Jesus Christ (1 Tim. 2. 5), standing at our side, does the Father's will and goes for-

[3] H. Engberding, 'Das chalkedonische Christusbild und die Liturgien der monophysitischen Kirchengemeinschaften' in *Das Konzil von Chalkedon*, II, Würzburg, 1953, pp. 697-733. This author correctly draws attention to the fact that the mode of speech corresponding to that movement of reaction did not remain confined within specifically monophysite circles.

[4] H. J. Schulz, 'Die "Höllenfahrt" also "Anastasis"' in *Zeitschrift für katholische Theologie*, LXXXI, 1959, pp. 1-66. Cf. Karl Rahner, 'Chalkedon Ende oder Anfang?' in *Das Konzil von Chalkedon*, II, Würzburg, 1954, pp. 3-49.

ward at the head of the human race to present the sacrifice
to his heavenly Father, is allowed to remain in the shadows,
even to become misunderstood.[5]

A well-balanced preaching of the faith will not neglect
these aspects, but will make an effort to see Christ the mediator as St Paul and, above all, the early Fathers saw him.
Both viewpoints converge when the mystery of Christ is
seen against the background of the mystery of the Trinity.
In this we are not thinking of the relationships within the
Trinity, which in this life we can grasp only in vague sur-
mise, but of the Trinity as revealed in the scheme of salvation, in the οἰκονομία.[6] In the Son God has entered this
world as man and has poured out his Spirit upon mankind.
Thus sanctified in the Holy Spirit, man returns to God the
Father, conducted by him who is his new Adam and High
Priest.[7] In this Christocentricity is only being deepened
once more; for Christ is our Redeemer only because he is
the bringer of grace and of the Holy Spirit.

These ideas were current among the Fathers of the first
centuries. They were constantly appearing right in the foreground. Nicetas of Remesiana (d. *c.* 414) concludes his
address to the newly baptized with these words: 'Because I
believe in the living God and his Christ, with whose Spirit I
am sealed, I have learned not to fear death at all.'[8] In the
third and fourth centuries the customary ending for liturgical prayer was an outburst of praise to the heavenly
Father, through Christ, in the Holy Spirit.[9]

---

[5] Schulz, pp. 50 f; O. Semmelroth, *Die Kirche als Ursakrament*, Frankfurt, 1953,
pp. 156–65.

[6] Thus in 'Christozentrik in der Verkündigung', pp. 4 f. (above p. 32, footnote
1), Ratzinger emphasizes that the Trinity as divine mystery is not a subject for
preaching. Trinitarian preaching can only be 'the exposition of the way of Christian
life through Christ, in the Spirit, to the Father.'

[7] Cf. I. Vagaggini, *Theologie der Liturgie*, Einsiedeln, 1959, p. 31.

[8] *De symbolo.*

[9] For example, in the Euchologion of Serapion (d. *c.* 360) a prayer over the newly
baptized concludes with an ascription of glory: '. . . to thee, the Creator of all,

If stressing Christocentricity is not to become a mere form of words, in particular if it is not to lead to an interchange of 'Christ' and 'God', then Christocentricity must be distinguished from theocentricity and not allowed to take its place. This follows from the fact that Christ ought to dominate the picture of the world of faith first and foremost as mediator. A mediator is a bridge linking two shores: in this case, God and mankind. On the one side is the infinite God, beginning and end of all things; on the other is mankind, far from God, but chosen by God and, as his Church, richly endowed with grace. To this extent it is perfectly correct to take the kingdom of God that has come in Christ as the central theme of the preaching of the faith.[10] This is simply to extend that which we have designated as the central point to cover the whole sphere which this central point illuminates. In a sense the kingdom of God embraces both shores: the sovereignty of God and this world which Christ has brought back home to God. Finally, as is self-evident, the holy God is that central point in which all searching and longing and striving must come to rest. Theocentricity is hence the primary law of the order of the world, and God is the goal of all the seeking and striving of his creatures.

The message of the faith comes to the aid of this seeking and striving by showing us the way in Christ. It is only because this too contains a multitude of statements that we designate as Christocentricity that central point which, within this multitude of statements, co-ordinates every-

---

through thy only begotten Son, Jesus Christ, through whom be honour and power to thee in the Holy Spirit, now and for ages of ages.' Cf. Jungmann, *Die Stellung Christi im liturgischen Gebet*, p. 23; pp. 130 ff. Cf. also the first Christmas sermon of Gregory the Great, still read at Matins of Christmas: *Agamus ergo, dilectissimi, gratias Deo Patri per Filium eius in Spiritu Sancto*.

[10] Th. Filthaut, *Das Reich Gottes in der katechetischen Unterweisung* (Untersuchungen zur Theologie der Seelsorge, XII, Freiburg, 1958, esp. pp. 194 ff.

thing in a unity. Christocentricity does not answer the same question as theocentricity. Theocentricity points to the ultimate goal of all striving; Christocentricity in the end gathers all directions about the way into a single sign-post.[11]

This indicates also the tremendous importance of the thought of God in all pastoral work. This importance does not apply to the little or much that we are able to say about God. Even by faith we can only stammer about God; even for faith God dwells in inaccessible light. Nevertheless he remains the centre around which our whole life revolves, the goal of all our searching, the end upon which all our paths must converge. To turn our eyes towards him, to keep the mind consciously and vigorously fixed upon him even in the darkness of this world, is and remains the ultimate aim of all religious and pastoral effort. The reason why the religious life is so weak in many of us may be because we orientate the metaphysical tension of human life too little towards God.[12] Hence we must do all we can to arouse and intensify the thought of God. In these days especially, in speaking of God we must not be slow to cull even from those things that the mind of man is able to know about God, so as to confirm and enrich the image of God that the faithful enjoy. This indeed may often be the unavoidable start of effective preaching.[13] Is it not merely the residue of

[11] A different language obviously arises if Christocentricity is predicated not of the ordering of the concepts of faith but of the order of the world itself. In the latter case the world is orientated towards Christ. Theocentricity and Christocentricity then become two concentric circles. This is the approach of K. Pfleger, *Die christozentrische Sehnsucht*, Colmar, undated. Cf. also Jungmann in *Zeitschrift für katholische Theologie*, LXVIII, 1944, pp. 107–9.

[12] It is worth noting that from his sixteenth year Cardinal Newman based his belief upon 'the thought of two and two only absolute and luminously self-evident beings, myself and my Creator.' *Apologia Pro Vita Sua*, London, 1890, p. 4, cf. also chap. 9.

[13] Cf. D. Grasso, *Il kerigma e la predicatione*, pp. 434 f. Grasso speaks of 'pre-evangelization' that is necessary in many cases, and mentions the remark of the French worker-priest, P. Loew: 'The vision of nature was the wave-length that put

our reaction against the age of apologetics, and a return to disguised traditionalism, such as characterized the early nineteenth century, that makes us often think that we may speak of God only in scriptural terms?

Scripture in fact presupposes natural knowledge of God. It directs us to it. One of the signs of man's present unnatural condition is his almost total blindness to God. In the twenty-first century men may perhaps indulge in psychological research to find out why in such a highly educated century as ours, not only the masses, but also many of the most outstanding intellects were no longer able to find a personal Creator behind this world of ever-increasing wonders. It is true that this decline in the knowledge of God has its reasons. We have explored this world and within it have uncovered an exhaustive interconnexion of all factors; we no longer recognize the voice of God in every peal of thunder, nor the touch of his hand in every extraordinary natural happening. To some extent God has been pushed away to the extreme edge of our experience. In addition, technical civilization has built a wall of human works around mankind, rendering us less and less sensitive to the language of nature which praises God. But there is gain here too. God is no longer 'the stop-gap in defective knowledge of nature' (H. U. v. Balthasar); he has become more, and where religion does exist it has become more genuine and purer.[14] For this reason therefore the task has once more fallen to preaching, of strengthening and clarifying the voice of nature which speaks, in every blade of grass and in every fibre of our bodies, of the omnipotent, ordering Spirit which has been at work there and still is at work. There is

us in touch with God.' The missionary-catechetical congress in Bangkok in 1962 correctly emphasized the fact that such a preparation for the Christian kerygma (pré-évangelisation) is specially necessary in missionary countries.

[14] Cf. K. Rahner, Schriften zur Theologie, iii, pp. 459 ff; A. Desqueyrat, La crise religieuse des temps nouveaux, 2nd ed., Paris, 1955, pp. 95 ff.

no need to elaborate proofs of God's existence in the pul-
pit; but where these are apparent we ought gladly to walk
in the tracks of the knowledge of God, thus learning and
teaching how to grasp and experience the nearness of God.
We may well be astonished at the intensity of the experience
of God which we detect in poets of our own century –
Rilke or Tagore; and even if we have to admit that frequently it is a pantheistic concept of God that we find
there, we must also affirm that we can and must experience
the nearness of the personal God in whom we live and move
and have our being (Acts 17. 27) with as great intensity as
do these poets. God is at once near and remote, the silent
God who throughout the centuries and millennia allows
men to grope for him in darkness, seeming to pay no heed to
their questions and appeals, their wandering and seeking.
But even in this the greatness and majesty of God becomes
manifest. 'This experience is basically nothing other than
the growth of God in the mind of mankind.'[15] It is a good
thing if our knowledge of God grows along these lines.
Amongst Christians we often find a truly miserable concept
of God, as though God were to be met only in church,
only in the tabernacle may be, as though, too, his chief
task were to answer our most idiotic desire the moment we
had expressed it in some petty prayer. Augustine, Ignatius
of Loyola, Newman, the Old Testament Psalmist, all the
great masters of prayer thought of God in a very different
way. Very different, too, was the notion of God held by the
Christians of the first centuries: we never find them making
any complaint that God not only leaves his faithful in all
generations exposed to all the world's oppression, but
also expects them to show life-long steadfastness in face of
persecution (1 Pet. 14. 17 ff.). They knew that God had
once broken his silence, and in his Son assured us once and

[15] Karl Rahner, *Schriften zur Theologie*, III, p. 461.

for all of his love, that his kingdom has already begun, although it is not yet perfected. They were prepared to look up in Christian hope to him who had created heaven and earth. Precisely if the faithful grasp and affirm the mysterious greatness of God, of which this world speaks in its own obscure language, will they be capable of judging what it means that the good news has been proclaimed to us from his lips in Christ.

VIII

Our Image of Christ

VERY LITTLE has been said about this, but in the past decades
signs have increased which show that the person of Christ
has once again come more into the forefront of Christian
consciousness. These signs have been connected not merely
with isolated cases but with the total life of the Church as
well. Since the time of Pius X the cult of saints has receded
even in the calendar of the universal Church. As recently
as fifty years ago a Sunday Mass could be displaced by any
saint's feast of double rank. This has been changed; even
in Lent saints' feast-days of this class need not affect the
Mass of the day, nor, after 1955, did they have to affect the
Office. Since the new regulations of 1960 they must not do
so.

The same tendency is to be seen in the arrangement of
churches. In the Baroque period people could not have
enough in the way of reliquaries, which were placed upon
the altar-table on feast-days; and the altar-piece whenever
possible had to portray dramatic scenes from the life of the
patron saint of the church; but now it is the crucifix, or a
representation of the Sacred Heart, or even a Pantokrator,
which dominates the space over the high altar. The encouragement of daily communion by Pius X, the biblical
movement, the liturgical movement, have all exerted an
effect along the same line. The feast of Christ the King was
established in 1925. In 1933, when Pius XI proclaimed a
jubilee year to commemorate the anniversary of our
redemption, it became clear that the emphasis upon the

mystery of Christ was directed not simply to our Lord's person, but also to his work.[1]

If here we have plain evidence of a return to an early Christian mode of thought, the contrast too must not be overlooked. This becomes especially clear against the background of the Apostles' Creed, a laconic confessional formula which comes near to poetry only when it mentions our Lord's triumph. Moeller is right when he says[2] that when reciting the Creed we practically come to a halt at *crucifixus est,* and simply allow our lips to move on to mention our belief in Easter, Ascension, and Pentecost. It is true that there is already a powerful movement at work which would go further – perhaps to overshoot the mark, a movement in which the Easter motif not only extends to include Pentecost, but would dominate Advent, reaching a final climax, through the thought of the Parousia, in Epiphany. That is to say, it would simply engulf the Christmas cycle.[3] It may well be that the warning of Pius XII in *Mediator Dei* against the one-sided cultivation of our Lord's glorified humanity was occasioned by such straining of what is a true realization.[4]

We dare not lose sight of the earthly life of Jesus, still less of the bitter sufferings and death by which our Lord wrought our redemption. Conversely, in the work of

[1] Until this date jubilee years had been related exclusively to the year of Christ's birth. Even Dionysius Exiguus had taken the birth of Christ as the beginning of the Christian era, whereas the Apostles' Creed had linked the historical anchoring of the redemptive events ('under Pontius Pilate') with the history of the Passion.

[2] *Lumen Vitae,* VII, 1952.

[3] On this view, the Christian Year would begin with Septuagesima. Cf. H. A. Reinhold, *The American Parish and the Roman Liturgy,* New York, 1958, pp. 116 ff. We cannot deny that such a view – supported by isolated examples from the history of the liturgy – has some justification. If we want to regard the Christian Year from the standpoint of the sanctification and perfection of the Church, we might well see Advent–Epiphany as its concluding phase. Because, however, the Church's Year is intended to be primarily a commemoration of the facts of redemption, it is more correct for it to begin with the *adventus Domini.*

[4] *A.A.S.,* XXXIX, 1947, pp. 579 f. Translation in *Christian Worship* (C.T.S., London, Do 270), p. 78, par. 216.

redemption we must not leave aside the Lord's resurrection either. This is more than the evidential seal upon Christ's words and deeds, provided for the convenience of apologetics. It is the visible acceptance of his redemptive passion by the heavenly Father. It is the victorious finale to the Passion-struggle, an image with which not only Paul and the Fathers loved to describe the work of redemption, but which remained right in the foreground until well on in the Middle Ages,[5] and which is being freshly appreciated here and there today.[6] The Resurrection itself is thus part of the redemptive happening, which is not exhausted in the concept of substitutionary satisfaction. At the same time it is also the first visible fruit of the redemption, the prototype of that new life which is the gift the redeemed are meant to receive.[7] Passion and Resurrection – following the early Christian pattern – ought to be viewed together. In this too our day has regained a few things. Without ignoring the terrible sufferings of our Lord, his crucified image is frequently represented today, as it was in Romanesque art, so as to express his triumphant lordship. In the new celebration of Easter, too, formerly separated into Holy Week and Easter, this unity has been restored, especially in the Easter Vigil.

In another respect, however, there is an instructive contrast between the attitude of the early Church and a

---

[5] Cf. the interpretation of Psalm 90. 3 by B. Fischer, 'Conculcabis leonem et draconem' in *Zeitschrift für katholische Theologie*, LXXX, 1958, pp. 421–9. The nun Hroswitha still regarded Christ as the champion (Gallicanus, Act III). Hugh of St Victor (d. 1141) is still placing Christ as champion theologically in the foreground: *De sacramentis christianae fidei* I, prol, 2 (*P. L.* CLXXVI, 183).

[6] The title of the third theological study-week, held in Rome in September 1957, was *Christus victor mortis*. Cf. the published referendum in *Gregorianum*, XXXIX, 1958, pp. 201–524.

[7] Thus the Resurrection is both *causa exemplaris* and *causa efficiens instrumentalis* of the redemption. The latter statement, adumbrated in the apostolic epistles and sermons, theologically formulated by St Thomas, has become the subject of closer discussion in modern theology. Cf. the congress in Rome (see previous note), especially the studies by S. Lyonnet and W. A. van Roo.

later attitude. In Western art since the late Middle Ages the Resurrection has regularly been treated as the joyful and consoling conclusion to the life of Jesus. As far as possible it is merely the historical event that is reproduced: the Lord in his glorified body rises up from the tomb, the guards fall back in fear, the angel proclaims the Resurrection. Interest may be aroused also by additional scenes of events between the Resurrection and the Ascension. Early Christian art dealt with the subject in quite a different way. It presented the resurrection of the Lord as the beginning of our resurrection.[8] To do this it employed veiled images, types of redemption, examples from Old Testament typology. It used direct statement also, as in the apse-pictures of the basilicas which portrayed Christ as the glorious ruler, surrounded by the apostles or holy martyrs, against a background of the heavenly Jerusalem.

To this day the Eastern Church, having survived transitory Western influences, recognizes as the true Easter-picture, besides that of the women at the tomb, only the picture described as a rule, misleadingly, as the Harrowing of Hell, wherein the risen Lord is seen grasping the hand of his forefathers – that is all mankind – and leading them up on high with him. In this way the Resurrection was raised out of its immediate significance as the concluding phase in the drama of our Lord's passion, and represented in its redemptive significance. Since then, indeed, Easter has been celebrated in this fashion; for from the earliest times Easter was also the festival of baptism, when the newly baptized were privileged to rise with Christ – a thought which today still dominates the liturgy of the whole of Easter week. The Introit recalls the picture of the passage through the Red Sea, of the land flowing with milk and honey, and sounds the call: *Venite benedicti*. Easter truly was the feast of the

[8] Cf. above, pp. 24-5.

redemption, and only as that feast could it be *the* feast (ἡ ἑορτή) as in the festival letters of St Athanasius. It is only because people saw in the resurrection of the Lord both the crowning of his redemptive sufferings and also the beginning of the new humanity that not only the annual commemoration of the Resurrection, but also its weekly commemoration has been kept, on Sunday as 'the Lord's day,' the day which preserves for the Christian the greatness and joy of his calling, and which is meant to confirm and strengthen him in that calling.

If the mystery of Christ contains the essential message of Christianity, because God has united all things in him (Eph. 1. 10); if, as St Paul desires, Christ is to live by faith within the hearts of the faithful (Eph. 3. 17), then it is obvious that a living Christianity would have to set about immediately and constantly to try to picture the figure of our Lord and all that this means for us as vividly and graphically as possible – even going beyond the immediate text of Scripture. In these attempts early Christianity in particular was not at all interested in recreating a picture of our Lord's earthly, historical appearance. St Paul himself had already assured us that it meant nothing to him to know Christ 'from a human point of view' (2 Cor. 5. 16). The mighty visions of St John, too, portray the Lord in the glory he had displayed on the mount of the Transfiguration (Apoc. 1. 9 ff.). His face is like the sun, his eyes flames of fire, his voice like the sound of many waters; he is the victorious lion of Juda (5. 5), the 'King of kings, and Lord of lords' (19. 16). The picture is through and through an Easter picture of Christ who has passed through his sufferings, who died but now lives for evermore (1. 18).

Nor was Christian art as it began to take shape in the second and third centuries concerned about the earthly Christ. In so far as it did not restrict itself to sheer symbolism – the sacred fish and later the Christ-monogram – it was satisfied with representational, symbolic pictures.[9] From the genre of the time they selected the picture of a shepherd carrying a lamb – the Christian knew what this meant, for catechesis had for long interpreted this as an image for salvation; or they portrayed the shepherd in the midst of his flock unrolling a parchment – the Christian is the pupil of 'the blessed shepherd who pastures his flock upon the hills and the plains' (Aberkios inscription); or they simply depicted a teacher, clothed in a pallium, seated, his right hand raised in instruction – again this is meant to indicate Christ, the Logos, understood as the one who, throughout the passing ages, and amidst the confusion of heathen opinions, brings salvation through the new knowledge of God; or a fisher is depicted casting his net in the water and 'luring the little fish with his sweet life' (Clement of Alexandria); or in a similar fashion one of the Old Testament types is reproduced. Under these and other images Christ was present in the mind of believers as the bringer of the new life in which they had come to share through baptism.

A change came about on the cessation of persecution under Constantine. The era of the now Christian empire saw the transference to Christ of predominantly sovereign attributes. Even the images of shepherd or teacher underwent reinterpretation along this line.[10] He is now the king, the victorious *imperator*; his head is adorned with a nimbus; he sits upon a royal throne or stands upon the clouds, his right hand raised in command; he is seen handing the roll of the law to Peter, as the emperor did when sending a high official off to the provinces. It is true that in the days of the

[9] On what follows cf. J. Kollwitz, *Das Christusbild des dritten Jahrhunderts,* Münster, 1953.

[10] J. Kollwitz, 'Das Bild von Christus dem König in Kunst und Liturgie der christlichen Frühzeit' in *Theologie und Glaube,* xxxviii, 1947–8, pp. 95–117.

struggle against the Arian heresy this preference for royal titles and royal imagery, like the advance of the ideas associated with Christmas and Epiphany, formed part of the Catholic insistence on the divinity of Christ. Clearly, as God, Christ is our absolute Lord and King; but at the same time the Easter victory which he had accomplished as God-man still stood in the front of the picture,[11] and this was frequently indicated explicitly by the addition of the cross, which surmounted the picture as a victory sign, in the form of the jewel-cross, or was given to the victor in the form of a light staff resembling a sceptre.

This era was followed by one of conservative tradition when the image of Christ as king remained dominant. Indeed, it became fixed as the *majestas Domini*. Even in Romanesque art this image frequently still dominated the space above the altar. It is significant that here the figure of our Lord is almost always surrounded by the four living creatures of Ezechiel – the man, the ox, the lion, the eagle – in allusion to the incarnation, the sacrificial death, the victorious resurrection, and the ascension of our Lord.[12] After this, however, the image of Christ crucified comes into its own as the standard image of Christ. This is not simply a process in the history of art. The transition was one of the results of the mighty revolution in medieval religious culture. As is well known, we find portrayals of the crucifixion in the art of the early Middle Ages, but these are seldom in a prominent place. Associated with an altar, and in favourite places in larger churches, the cross occasionally appears. From the Carolingian period onwards it appears with

[11] J. Kollwitz, *Das Bild*, pp. 115 ff.
[12] K. Künstle, *Ikonographie der christlichen Kunst*, I, Freiburg, 1928, pp. 603–12. Künstle shows that this was the original interpretation of these four symbols, not yet wholly forgotten in the Middle Ages. 'The allusion to the evangelists is but one of the many artificialities of allegory . . . it would have been an unusual honour for the four evangelists' (pp. 611 f.).

increasing frequency.[13] The glorification of the cross is one of the chief motifs in Alcuin's piety and poetry.[14] The Roman–German *Pontificale* of Mainz (c. 950) shows the veneration of the holy cross on Good Friday already developed as a great rite around which private devotion had wound its tendrils: for each of the three double genuflexions with which one approached the cross, special and extensive prayers were provided, greetings of the holy cross such as we now find in every collection of prayers.[15]

After the eleventh century it became more and more usual for every altar to be adorned with a crucifix; by the end of the Middle Ages this became a fixed law; and very soon it had become part of the furniture of every monastic cell.[16] The crucifix became identical with the image of Christ, Romanesque art was able, nevertheless, to handle the subject not naturalistically, so as to portray only the dying, or dead, Redeemer, but so as truly to represent the mystery of Christ. The Resurrection-victory is suggested as well. The Crucified is in an almost standing posture, the crown of thorns has become a royal crown, and the linen robe a flowing mantle, and the accompanying figures – Mary, John, or a symbolic figure – often indicate the fruits of the redemption, that is the Church.

Not until the Gothic period in Church art was the context of the economy of redemption lost to sight. Religious art then became content to portray, in a more or less noble style, the doleful, pitiable condition of the suffering Redeemer, and, by this representation of what had once happened, to evoke pious sympathy. In this form, or in a

[13] J. Braun, *Der christliche Altar*, 1, Munich, 1924, pp. 401–5.

[14] H. B. Meyer, *Alkuin*, pp. 341–3; *idem.*, 'Crux decus es mundi. Alkuins Kreuz- und Osterfrömmigkeit' in *Paschatis Sollemnia*, ed. B. Fischer and J. Wagner, Freiburg, 1959, pp. 96–107.

[15] E. Dumoutet, *Le Christ selon la chair et la vie liturgique au moyen-âge*, Paris, 1932, pp. 16 ff.

[16] Dumoutet, pp. 23 ff.

form only very slightly modified by the sentiments of later generations, the crucifix came to be, and remains, the symbol and summary of the Christian faith. In this form we find it in churches and chapels, at wayside shrines, and upon mountain-tops; thus it sanctifies Christian homes and adorns the graves of the faithful, and in our times the battle to preserve Christian education for our children is a battle for the retention of the crucifix on the school-room wall.

As we have already mentioned, this historical and narrative representation of the cross expresses the most decisive and central fact in the Christian message, but not the whole of that message. Moreover, a presupposition of prayerful adoration is that the worshipper transpose himself into the past, into the hours of the Passion, for the Christ of the present, whom our prayer is supposed to reach, is not the suffering Christ, but Christ risen and sitting at the right hand of the Father.[17] Room had been left, therefore, for a fresh approach.

And so, even in the declining Middle Ages, we find the beginnings of a new image of Christ, an image that has pressed more and more into the foreground in the course of the past few centuries, finally entering into competition with the crucifix.[18] This is the image of the Sacred Heart of Jesus. In this image – a sculptured or painted figure of our Lord, his heart visible upon his breast and bearing the symbols of suffering love, the wounds in the side, the crown

---

[17] Cf. Karl Rahner, *Schriften zur Theologie*, III, p. 411: 'Prayer addressed to the suffering Saviour is, from the theological point of view, prayer to the Christ who has suffered.'

[18] This could be felt when at the turn of last century the movement for the 'enthronement of the Sacred Heart' began. Among other things this movement advocated the setting up of a Sacred Heart Picture before the assembled family. The Sacred Heart was being given the place traditionally accorded to the crucifix. An attempt at fusion was made by depicting a heart upon the breast of the Crucified, as in the crucifix by Joseph Bachlechner above the high altar in the Canisianum at Innsbruck. There is an account of the difficulties that were then overcome in the correspondence of the *Priestergebetsverein*, LXIV, Innsbruck, 1929–30, p. 134.

of thorns, flames of fire – adoration of Christ in recent times has found its favourite expression. There can be no doubt that in recent centuries this devotion has been one of the great restorative powers in the life of the Church. For countless numbers of people devotion to the Sacred Heart, along with their consciously learned knowledge and obedient practice of the faith, has led them to the point where faith has sprung to life as the revelation of the redeeming love of God, and as stimulus to a sacrificial Christian life. The hundreds of religious societies, the thousands of Church organizations which have done unselfish charitable work or spent all their energies in the work of education, the apostolate, the missions, under the banner of the Sacred Heart, are the best proof of that.

Various energies have contributed to the formation of this symbol, which in God's providence has been turned to such good purpose. In every age the word 'heart' has been an expression of endearment and of primary value; but the 'mythology of the heart' was specially in tune with culture at the beginning of the modern epoch; for this was an epoch which held feeling and sentiment in high esteem. At the same time it was a period when the Christian doctrines of salvation had come to be conceived more in systematic terms than in the language of salvation-history, more in theological than in biblical terms. It was a period which even in a comprehensive symbol was perfectly happy to include a multiplicity of separate symbols, such as the wounds, the thorns, the cross, and fire, all assimilated to the symbol of the heart. It was quite natural for this period ultimately to superimpose all of these symbols upon the earthly figure of the Saviour. People were all the more receptive to such a combination because the portrayals of the Crucified – as we have noted – had been devised more as an isolated excerpt from the total process of salvation-history. Thus the symbol of the heart was a welcome expression that gathered up all the complexities of theological systems and difficulties, of apologetic distinctions, vividly illustrating what was most vital: that God is love and calls us to himself, full of compassion, and that he is worthy of all our love. In addition this symbol by its sheer concentration served as the sharpest possible antithesis to the severity of Jansenism, as also to the cold rationalism of the Enlightenment and the godlessness of rising secularism.

On the other hand, it is significant that almost every major work of the copious literature on devotion to the Sacred Heart, written during the past century – including papal encyclicals – begins with an apology. Today no one can shut his eyes to the fact that this devotion, in so far as it feels that it has to stress our Lord's physical heart, encounters many difficulties, especially for young people, and that these difficulties have increased since the end of the Second World War. An age that has known such devastation, that turns instinctively – as a result of the rule of empiricism in science – to what is tangible and verifiable, that has become accustomed by technical civilization to sober, factual thinking, does not take kindly to symbolism that relies upon feeling and sympathy, especially as the literary or artistic presentation of this symbolism so often offends good taste.

There is another side to the picture too. In the religious education of youth, renewed emphasis upon salvation-history in the catechism, the attempt to portray the complete biblical, Pauline image of Christ in the minds of the young, and education through the liturgy with its prayer 'through Christ' and the revived Easter cycle, have all helped to create a new atmosphere. New approaches have been opened up into the mystery of Christ, approaches which seem to be in harmony with the oldest Christian tradition. And so many have gained the impression that if, as devotion to the Sacred Heart stresses, God's compassionate love has come down to us in Christ, then this must indeed be contained in an even more immediate fashion in those rediscovered sources which were the original records of that love, and the responsive love which this modern devotion evokes cannot have been lacking in the Church of the martyrs.

We shall have to concede that Catholic piety, as it emerges today out of the various revival movements, has regained or at least made accessible once more the very thing that is really meant by devotion to the Sacred Heart, but it presents it in another form and derives it from other sources. Even so, we are still far from having exhausted the possibilities.

Devotion to the Sacred Heart will not, however, disappear from the life of the Church; but if it is to be and to remain 'the synthesis of all religion,'[19] it cannot avoid undergoing some further development; and this will not be the first development that it has known.[20] It has already been asserted several times that the presentation of the devotion by Pius XII in *Haurietis aquas,* in contrast to Pius XI and Leo XIII, stresses the biblical basis rather than the private revelation, and that even the idea of reparation to the Sacred Heart is not stressed in the same way as it was by Pius XI.

Liturgical formularies have always attempted to provide a certain broadening of the perspectives of the notion of the Sacred Heart in respect of its biblical basis. The stylistic law of the liturgy itself demanded that this should be so. A similar expansion, however, had to come about in the extra-

[19] Pius XI in *Miserentissimus Redemptor: A.A.S.,* xx, p. 167: *'totius religionis summa.'* Repeated by Pius XII in *Haurietis aquas: A.A.S.,* xlviii, 1956, p. 313.

[20] This can be seen in the considerable number of different versions of the Sacred Heart Mass that have appeared in the course of time. Before Pius XI prescribed a formulary for this there were at least thirteen. Cf. N. Nilles, *De rationibus festorum SS. Cordis Jesu et purissimi Cordis Mariae,* ii, 5th ed., Innsbruck, 1885, pp. 1–42.

liturgical forms of the devotion, especially in so far as these were intended for common use. This development, this 'Churching' of the devotion, is already in progress. 'This devotion is now on the way to an undreamed-of theological deepening; more and more it is becoming what solicitous criticism has been demanding and expecting of it: it is becoming more scriptural, more theological, more liturgical.'[21] In the Sacred Heart devotion too we must never forget that Christ is the mediator; and the trinitarian overall structure of the Christian order of redemption must not be ignored.[22]

The need of atonement need not be suppressed. Reparation is an indispensable element of genuine spiritual life. At the same time we must note that, although it may not be dogmatically false, it is kerygmatically inappropriate to offer atonement to Christ the Lord who himself became the atonement for our sins (1 John 2. 2) instead of to the triune God who is offended by sin.[23] It is perfectly consonant with the essential warmth of the devotion to the Sacred Heart to relate the love of the heart of the Redeemer not so much to the individual, to the isolated worshipper – as is perhaps implied in visions and private revelations – as to see it as a world-wide redemptive love, the first fruit of which is the Church – *ex corde scisso Ecclesia* – as members of which we receive grace and salvation.[24] Justice would be done to

---

[21] Hugo Rahner, 'Mirabilis progressus' in *Cor Jesu*, 1, Rome, 1959, p. 53.

[22] Karl Rahner, *Schriften zur Theologie*, iii, pp. 391–415. Rahner sums up his statements by saying 'that the basic religious and kerygmatic formula is not "towards Christ", but "with him and in him (incorporated in his life and death) towards the Father"' (p. 402).

[23] Karl Rahner, *Schriften zur Theologie*, iii, p. 408. Even the encyclical *Miserentissimus Deus* finally makes this transition in its elaboration of the notion of atonement. *A.A.S.*, xx, 1928, pp. 169 ff.

[24] We must see the proposal in 1900 of many Church leaders to inaugurate a 'feast of the social kingdom of the Sacred Heart' as an attempt along these lines. This formula bore all too clearly the mark of compromise. C. Noppel, 'Das soziale Königtum Christi' in *Stimmen der Zeit*, cix, 1925, pp. 241–8. The idea behind this was later given its proper place through the institution of the feast of Christ the King.

all of these factors if we took as our symbol, not so much the image of an isolated heart, as the image from the climax of salvation-history – the heart of Jesus pierced with a lance, from which flowed blood and water. The pictorial representation of this could be an accentuation of this feature of the crucifix, as has always been to some extent the intention of Christian art,[25] or it could be the portrayal of the risen Lord with this feature somehow suggested, thus returning to the basic motif of early Christian iconography.

It is now logical to conclude that the theology of the Sacred Heart ought no longer to find its place as a kind of apologetic appendix in connexion with the adorability of the person of Christ, but that it ought rather to be found as 'the crown and conclusion of Christology,'[26] if not in fact at the conclusion of soteriology.

In this way devotion to the Sacred Heart will no longer stand out in such sharp relief as something quite special, because other methods of devotion have been opened up and, above all, the freshly understood primitive Catholic form of the liturgical veneration of the mystery of Christ has regained much of its original richness. Rather, it is to be understood as a great triumph for the Sacred Heart devotion that its spirit is beginning to penetrate other forms of piety, even those which make little or no mention of a heart; and furthermore it will be the task of this devotion, under the symbol of this Heart, to work for the preservation and increase in the Church of its own lively spirit. Its root in the liturgy, through the feast of the Sacred Heart and the monthly emphasis on the first Friday – a day which the Church has always observed as the day of redeeming love

[25] As is well known, the ancient, traditional portrayal of the lance-wound in the right side of the Crucified goes back to the idea that this wound opened up the fountain that Ezechiel prophesied would arise at the right side of the temple (Ezech. 47. 1 f.; cf. John 2. 19 – Christ is the temple).

[26] K. Wittkemper, discussing the dogmatics of Pohle-Gierens, II, 10th ed., in *Theol. Revue*, LIII, 1957, p. 74.

and of atoning participation (fasting) – will provide this devotion with a permanent, sure foundation.[27]

In every form of the image of Christ, traditional or modern, in all forms of prayer and devotion in which the motif of the mystery of Christ is displayed, in all our preaching of the faith, in every thing which speaks of Christ, we must be at pains to ensure that the mighty context of salvation-history is not falsified, and that the central events of salvation-history are not understood in a merely juridical way. Redemption is more than the creation of a new legal relationship between God and man. Clement of Alexandria spoke of a κοσμικὸς ἀγών, a cosmic tournament which Christ has fought and won. By his victorious battle the world has been transformed and man's life given a new foundation.

It is surely of the greatest importance today that these broad contours of the Christian order of redemption and of the world, and this manly tone of the Christian message, in contrast to all feeble emasculations, be allowed more and more to gain the upper hand.[28]

[27] It is astonishing, therefore, that today we hear suggestions that Friday fasting should be abolished. If it were, not only would a piece of ancient Christian discipline be abandoned, but a firm support of the Christian consciousness of faith would be taken away. Cf. Jungmann, 'Der Christliche Freitag' in *Festschrift für P. Thomas Michels*, 1961.

[28] Cf. St. Grün, *Verkündigung in der Glaubenskrise der Zeit*, Würzburg, 1956, pp. 81 ff. With special reference to the presentation of redemption, Grün emphasizes that Christianity must become apparent 'in its essential, cosmic, and militant greatness' (p. 92).

IX

The Cult of Mary

THE MARIAN motif is inextricably bound up with Christology. We call Mary the 'mother of God' because she bore
him who is the true God. This is a title of honour which is
due to Mary, but is not the comprehensive definition of her
place in the order of redemption and in devotion. It is,
however, a possible starting-point for Christian piety, as
the history of Eastern piety is the first to demonstrate. The
battle against the heresy of Arius and its offshoots led to the
emphasis being placed, in the new Chalcedonian formula,
upon the divinity of Christ, by which his human nature was
encompassed and permeated. And so the phrase 'Christ our
God' became a constant expression in prayer. If Christ thus
came to be seen and worshipped predominantly as at God's
right hand, as God himself, indeed; if man's sight of his
mediatorial office was blinded by the glare of his divinity,
then it was the θεοτόκος alone who could now provide
mediation between the sinful human world and the divine
Son, in the minds of the faithful.

In the East this led to a proliferation of many striking
creations. Every canonical Hour in the Byzantine rite
concludes with a Theotokion, a hymn to the mother of
God. Within the Byzantine Mass, immediately after the
consecration and epiclesis – as in the Latin *Communicantes*
where Mary is named first in the list of saints – Mary is
described as 'the all-holy, immaculate, honourable, and
glorious mistress, the God-bearer and ever-virgin,' and then
this declaration winds up, right in the middle of the Canon
of every Mass, with a hymn in praise of Mary – the *Megaly-*

narion. The Marian feature is to be found even more strongly accentuated in that form of Christianity which so exaggerated the divinity of Christ that it became heretical: the monophysitism of the Copts and the Ethiopians. In this milieu there grew up such a tremendous wealth of Marian poetry that no theologian writing a Marian tractate ever fails to draw copiously from it. The Ethiopian liturgy has even produced a so-called Marian Anaphora, a Mass formulary, every prayer of which is addressed to Mary. When in modern times the Jesuits went to Abyssinia to work for reunion, their opponents charged them with being the enemies of Mary.[1] This charge continues to be laid against the members of all non-monophysite Churches.[2]

The rise of the cult of Mary in the East soon began to affect the West, where devotional life, especially in the Gallican region, showed a similar if somewhat weaker reaction to Arianism, and hence had begun to follow a similar course. In the sixth and seventh centuries the four great Eastern Marian feast-days had taken root in the West also. These feasts were: the Nativity of our Lady, Candlemas, the Annunciation, and the Assumption. Eastern Marian ikons had spread everywhere, and even today these often bear the Greek letters M(ήτη)P Θ(εο)Υ. Eastern Marian poetry was taken as a model. Since the eleventh century this has been specially true of the renowned hymn *Akathistos* – a long series of ejaculations to Mary, each beginning with Χαῖρε, and followed by some new title of honour. By replacing the Χαῖρε at the beginning of the verse with an *Ora pro nobis* at the end, the Marian litanies of the late Middle Ages and finally the Litany of Loreto were formed.[3]

[1] A. Mendez, *Expeditionis Aethiopicae*, l. 2, Rome, 1908, p. 329.

[2] M. A. van den Oudenrijn, 'De cultu B. Mariae Virginis apud Aethiopes' in *Angelicum*, XXXVII, 1960, pp. 3–18, esp. pp. 12 f. This author, in contrast to the many admirers of Ethiopian Marian devotion, paints a critical picture of it.

[3] G. G. Meersseman, *Der Hymnos akathistos im Abendland,* Freiburg, Switzerland, 1958.

In the West, too, from about the end of the tenth century the tide of Marian devotion rose mightily. In the West it now became customary to conclude each Hour of the Divine Office with a Marian antiphon similar to the Theotokion of the East. Not only in popular devotions, but in many local versions of the Roman liturgy the *Ave Maria* became an almost indispensable extension of the *Pater noster* in various places, as, for example, in the Preces, in the liturgy of baptism, and even in various interpolations in the Mass.[4] There are isolated cases of the same thing happening to the *Gloria Patri* at the end of the psalms.[5] On Marian feast-days even the *Gloria in excelsis* was given a Marian interpolation: *Tu solus sanctus Mariam sanctificans, Tu solus Dominus Mariam gubernans. . . .* The reforms that began with the Council of Trent saw these as obvious accretions and cut many of them out. But the retrograde movement was by no means halted. The much-needed reform of the calendar under Pius X deprived the four ancient Marian feasts of their status as holidays of obligation. The rubrical reform of 1955 not only abolished two Marian octaves and restricted the use of the Marian antiphons, but – quite astonishingly – expunged every *Ave Maria* from the Breviary.

These diminutions, balanced by increases elsewhere, were certainly not intended to lead to any denial of the veneration of our Lady; but in some measure the cult has been diverted from a development more in tune with Eastern piety, and brought back into line with the Western–Roman tradition. The development of late medieval popular devotion was well upon the way to substituting a mediation through Mary to Jesus (or God) for the mediation through Christ to God. At all events it was prepared to see in Mary the figure

---

[4] Cf. Jungmann, *The Mass of the Roman Rite*, London, 1959, p. 466.

[5] Drontheimer Missal of 1519 (H. Fahn, *Fire norske Messeordninger*, Oslo, 1953, pp. 22 and 42).

to whom our eyes must turn when we look towards God.[6]
St Bernard had already taken the first step along this road
when, in his sermon on our Lady's assumption, he said that
we need a mediator with the Mediator. We find this in Mary
in whom is no severity or terror, and whom human
weakness can approach without fear.[7] This idea becomes
even more distinct later. We often hear it said, even down
to the present day, that Christ (although we have been in-
grafted into him through baptism as a branch on a vine) is
all too far from us, all too divine; and so, statements, which
apply to him as the God-man, the new Adam, the prototype
of mankind in grace, are transferred to Mary who, as
purely human, stands closer to us; then *she* becomes the
prototype of the new humanity. Although these statements
may not be incorrect, and, in a certain context, make sense,[8]
if used constantly they may lead to error and arouse justifiable opposition.[9] At all events, the cause of such transference is not above suspicion: it is the uneasiness about
taking the human nature of Jesus Christ, the God-man, in
earnest. And yet he himself wanted that humanity to be our

[6] A man was knighted 'to the honour of God and Mary.' The sequence *Deo
omnipotenti, B. Mariae semper Virgini* had become fixed in the *Confiteor*. Against this
cf. 1 Tim. 5. 21; 6. 13. While this manner of speaking obviously has its place, from
the kerygmatic point of view it is a shade less suitable when God and his mother
are spoken of in one breath, as is done occasionally, and not just in popular language.
Cf. a eulogy of Pius XII reported in the *Österreichischen Archiv für Kirchenrecht*, IX,
1958, p. 241: *pietate impensissima erga Deum eiusque Virginem Matrem enituit.* The title of
an otherwise admirable book by F. G. Holweck is in the same strain: *Calendarium
liturgicum festorum Dei et Dei Matris Mariae,* Philadelphia, 1925.

[7] Migne, *P. L.* CLXXXIII, 429 f. Cf. H. Holstein, 'Du véritable amour envers
Notre Dame' in *Christus*, IX, 1945, pp. 60–75, esp. 69 ff.

[8] The Danish convert Peter Schindler (*Das Netz des Petrus*, Regensburg, 1957,
p. 279) makes the pertinent comment that if Mary is called *vita dulcedo et spes nostra*
'that is as though I were to tell my own mother that she is the sweetest, most
beautiful, and wisest woman upon earth.' It is simply an expression of love.

[9] It is well known that the Reformers, Luther in particular, protested vehemently
against this analogous transference to Mary of the predicates belonging to Christ.
The above-mentioned (n. 3) *akathistos* hymn, and its Western derivatives, contain
an extraordinary multiplication of such transferences.

primary model.[10] This tendency is the disguised, unconscious monophysitism of which we spoke earlier.[11]

In this way forms of devotion thrive which may give outsiders the impression that Catholic Christianity is more a Madonna-cult than the worship of the Blessed Trinity.[12] These forms of devotion were nourished by Marian literature which undoubtedly revealed a tendency to divinize Mary, because it was aimed, one-sidedly, at stressing her personal privileges,[13] viewing Mary as an 'autonomous entity within salvation-history.'[14] Similar dangers obviously face the attempts to highlight the personal privileges of St Joseph by the construction of a special Josephology.[15]

It is an encouraging sign that in these days efforts are increasingly being made to integrate the Marian motif within the total picture of the Christian order of salvation.

[10] Cf. Karl Rahner, *Theological Investigations*, I, pp. 149–200: 'Current Problems in Christology'. 'As true Man, who, standing before God on our side in free human obedience, is Mediator, . . .' (p. 161). Jesus is the man 'whose life is one of absolutely unique self-oblation to God' (p. 172). B. Poschmann, too, *Theol. Revue*, XLIV, 1948, p. 46, stresses, against H. Koster, that it is primarily Christ and not Mary who represents humanity, even in the receptive sense.

[11] Above, pp. 38 f. With perfect logicality the monophysite Church of Ethiopia has developed a litany in which Christ is addressed 'through Mary.' S. Grébaut, *Aethiopica*, III, 1935, pp. 145–53; cf. *Jahrbuch für Liturgiewissenschaft*, XV, 1941, p. 450.

[12] Cf. G. Papini, *Papst Cölestin VI, Briefe an die Menschen*, Vienna, 1948, pp. 33 f. There is a type of pastoral care which sees its task simply as the protection and cultivation of forms of devotion that are current among a section of the faithful who still live within a complacent tradition. This arises entirely from the refusal to address that very group who live within the intellectual world of our day and upon whom the future depends. Cf. P. Fransen, 'Die erste Session des Konzils' in *Wort und Wahrheit*, XVIII, 1963, pp. 9–24: 'The representatives of this view have lost all living contact with the intellectuals in their own countries. At best they may have preserved faith in the masses, but they fail to see that even the faith of these is threatened by the spirit of our times' (p. 20).

[13] An extreme case of such divinization is provided, for example, by studies which consider the sort of knowledge which our Lady possessed at the moment of her conception: cf. *Marianum*, XVII, 1955, pp. 473–526.

[14] A. Müller, 'Fragen und Aussichten der heutigen Mariologie' in *Fragen der Theologie heute*, Einsiedeln, 1957, p. 315. Müller comments that the impression is given that 'Mary's co-redemption of us is greater than our redemption by Christ.'

[15] The *Sociedad Ibero-Americana de Josefologia* held its fifth *Semana de Estudios Josefinos* in Valladolid from April 20–3, 1960. In 1961 the *Cahiers de Josephologie* celebrated its ninth anniversary.

Mary is viewed along with the Church; she is the first-redeemed of redeemed humanity. It is made plain that Mary and the Church are a single mystery, worked out in two forms: 'the mystery of man's redemption in Christ, sent by God, received and taken up by men, and handed on throughout the history of mankind.'[16] To regard Mary and the Church as thus related is only to take up once again the Marian devotion of the Fathers, above all of Augustine, and of a tradition that was very much alive until the eighth century.[17]

Finally, this cycle of ideas is suggested in the Apostles' Creed where the words with which the Christ-kerygma begins: 'conceived of the Holy Spirit, born of the Virgin Mary' corresponds, as an exact parallel, to the words with which the list of the treasures of redemption begins: 'I believe in the Holy Spirit, the holy Catholic Church.'[18] It is only after a thousand years have passed that predicates, customarily applied to holy Church (or the individual soul), and even more, the laudatory imagery used to describe the bride of the Song of Songs, were transferred, at first predominantly, then exclusively, to our Lady.[19] It is obvious that here the horizons will have to be widened and the essentials brought into the foreground once more.[20]

On the other hand it is self-evident that the return to a

[16] A. Müller, p. 309. Cf. *id.*, *Ecclesia–Maria*, Fryburg, 1951.

[17] H. Coathalem, *Le parallélisme entre la Sainte Vierge et l'église dans la tradition latine*, Rome, 1954.

[18] It is even plainer in the older so-called Re-form of the Creed: *qui natus est de Spiritu Sancto et Maria Virgine. Et in Spiritum Sanctum, sanctam Ecclesiam.*

[19] J. Beumer, 'Die marianische Deutung des Hohenliedes in der Frühscholastik' in *Zeitschrift für katholische Theologie*, LXXVI, 1954, pp. 411–39; also H. de Lubac, *The Splendour of the Church*, London, 1956, pp. 240–70.

[20] A group of young girls, dedicated to the work of the apostolate, presented the superiors of several religious houses with a questionnaire. This shows how strong the feeling for such things has grown even an the best strata of Catholic youth. '6. Who and what stands at the centre of the devotional life of your order? In the month of March is it St Joseph or Lent? In May is it Mary or Easter? 7. Is Advent regarded as the true month of Mary?' *Geist und Leben*, XXXIV, 1961, p. 137.

harmonious integration of Mariological ideas does not mean a denial of essential forms of the Marian devotion which has for long found its home within the Church. It does mean, however, that Marian devotion, with its warmth of feeling and winning power, should remain true to the over-all picture of Christian doctrine, and, conversely, that this devotion should itself receive clarification and theological stability from doctrine. In the end it is the mystery of Christmas that will thus be more deeply grasped; and the contemplation of this mystery is bound to lead to awestruck praise of the virgin-mother, as the liturgy has demonstrated from time immemorial, answering one of the Christmas Eve lessons with its: *Sancta et immaculata virginitas, quibus te laudibus efferam nescio.* With the same intention Michael Schmaus says that Mariology is 'Christology unfolded.'[21] What we advocate here is the kerygmatic integration of the Marian motif too, an integration and total conception that may well result in a certain selection from the too rich forms of the cult of Mary, but which will result in further development as well.

[21] M. Schmaus, *Katholische Dogmatik*, v, Munich, 1955, p. 5.

X

Holy Church

THE CHURCH herself is still in need of kerygmatic integration. It is not very long since one was accustomed to see the Church simply as a hierarchical entity, the God-given organization which held the faithful together by her authority, and offered them the means of salvation. Corresponding to this was the view that the faithful did indeed come to the Church, and were cared for by the Church, but little thought was given to the fact that they too are the Church. A change has been going on for a long time in all this, but it is still a long way from having permeated the general consciousness. One decisive aspect of the change is seen in the way that theological manuals no longer treat of the Church, of ecclesiology, in a purely apologetic manner. As is fitting the Church is treated dogmatically and represented as the link between the doctrine of redemption and the doctrine of grace. Above all the Church is the community of the redeemed; for this reason it is possible to view together Mary, as the first-redeemed, and the Church. Redemption is laid down by God first of all in the Church. God's gracious call has gone out to mankind – *in omnem terram* – and from this call comes the assembling of the called, the *Ecclesia*, the first and last predicate of which is the holiness which is election: *sancta Ecclesia* (ἀγία εκκλησία = κλητοὶ ἅγιοι). For it is not through faith, but primarily through the sacramental sign, the *sigillum fidei,* that is performed in the name of the Church, and through which the individual is received into the redemptive community of the Church, that one receives salvation.

'For the elect, salvation consists in being welcomed, for good and all, into the heart of the Church.'[1]

The reason for the Church's being the bringer of salvation, the ark of redemption, is that Christ lives on in her in his divine nearness, his fullness of grace, his power to sanctify. She is 'a reality that flows out from Christ in every present moment of her life, . . . the pulse of an ever-living heart that beats throughout the history of the world.'[2] Her purpose is to enable all who come to her and belong to her to share more and more in the riches of Christ, thus making possible and fostering that transformation and new creation in the image of Christ (cf. Rom. 8. 29), that 'putting on of Christ' (Gal. 3. 27), of which the apostle speaks. 'The Church's unique mission is that of making Christ present to men. She is to announce him, show him, and give him, to all.'[3] And so she is not only the bride of Christ, but his body as well, the *corpus Christi mysticum*. Where people have a lively awareness of this concept, the Church without more ado fits into a Christocentric system of faith.

Obviously we have to distinguish between the Church as the total number of the faithful united within her, and the Church in her hierarchical structure. In the first sense she is the *plebs sancta,* the *communio sanctorum* as expressed in the current form of the Apostles' Creed, where these phrases are added in explanation after *sancta Ecclesia catholica*.[4]

It is precisely the changing interpretation which in the course of the centuries has been put upon the phrase 'the communion of saints' that demonstrates the change to

---

[1] H. de Lubac, *The Splendour of the Church*, London, 1956, p. 40.

[2] P. Lippert, *Die Kirche Christi*, Freiburg, 1931, p. 202.

[3] H. de Lubac, *The Splendour of the Church*, p. 161.

[4] The expression *communio sanctorum,* κοινωνια τῶυ ἁγίων, belongs, as we know, to later sources too, where it usually possesses the abstract meaning of sharing in (what is holy). Cf. the relevant article in *Lexikon für Theologie und Kirche*, IV, 1960, pp. 651–3; VI, 1961, pp. 410 f. The context of the Apostles' Creed corresponds to the concrete meaning that the Church is the community of the sanctified.

which the understanding of the Church has been subjected. As early as Alcuin the communion of saints no longer denotes the whole Church which is holy in all of her members through the grace of Christ, but only the triumphant Church of the perfect.[5] Until recently our catechisms understood the communion of saints almost universally as the union or community of possession between the faithful on earth, the saints in heaven, and the holy souls in purgatory.[6] Not until this century did a few catechisms, including to some extent the German Cathechism of 1955, return to the original full notion of the communion of saints – as indeed the Roman Catechism had done.

The Church is the community of saints; but because the Church is an ordered society she cannot be conceived without her hierarchical structure, without the equipment of offices and powers provided by Christ himself. The cause of the temporary obscuring of the nature of the Church was merely the one-sided emphasis upon, and isolated consideration of, the official side of the Church, principally of her pastoral office – an emphasis occasioned by the circumstances of the time. It is perfectly clear that the teaching office, the priestly office, and the pastoral office are not autonomous distinctions for particular persons; they are meant to be related to the Church as the totality of the faithful, for whose benefit they are provided. These offices are nothing other than the continuance and extension of the tasks which the God-man took up on our behalf. The infallible teaching office of the Church perpetuates his doctrinal wisdom. Priestly activity is possible in the Church only to the extent that the priest acts as the organ, the instrument, of the High Priest; and the pastoral office preserves in its very name, as in the symbolic crozier of the bishop, the image of the Good

---

[5] H. B. Meyer, *Alkuin*, pp. 419 f.
[6] M. Ramsauer, *Die Kirche in der Katechismen*, pp. 323 f.; pp. 336 ff.

Shepherd, in whose name alone authority in the Church can be exercised. It is one and the same God-man who continues to live both in the life of grace of the faithful, and in the powers of ecclesiastical authority. Ecclesiastical authority need not stand in sharp antithesis to the laity in the Church. The official ministry in the Church leads along the way of salvation, a way that we all must travel. The pastoral office itself demands not only the obedience of the faithful, but their co-operation also (Catholic Action). Teaching likewise ought not only to be imparted by official catechists, but ought also to be handed on by Christian parents to the rising generation. Indeed doctrine ought not simply to be held by each of the faithful: it ought to be manifested by him in his environment.

Above all it is the priesthood, in its expression as presbyterate and episcopate, that is reserved for special officials. It is significant, however, that the Scriptures ascribe the priesthood primarily to the whole of the faithful, that is to the Church (1 Pet. 2. 5; Apoc. 1. 6). All who belong to Christ, all who have become joined to him through faith and baptism, are empowered to approach God in him and with him. Through Christ they have access – προσαγωγή – to the throne of God (Rom. 5. 2; Eph. 2. 18), which formerly was closed to men. They exercise their priesthood most fully when, in the assembly of the Church, they join in presenting the sacrifice of the Eucharist. It is true that they are not presbyters, and they need the services of the presbyter, if they wish to appear as priests before God in the holy sacrifice; but they are as close to God as the presbyters are.[7] It is quite unnecessary for us constantly to use the

[7] H. de Lubac, *The Splendour of the Church*, pp. 92–101 f. There is but a single priesthood in the Church. The sacrament of holy order does not create two grades of belonging to Christ. Cf. E. Niebecker, *Das allgemeine Priestertum der Gläubigen*, Paderborn, 1936; V. Ordóñez, 'El sacerdocio de los fideles' in *Revista Española de Teologia*, XVI, 1956, pp. 359–79.

word 'priesthood' to express this dignity of the Christian, especially as the word has come to be used normally in its narrower connotation. Besides this it is derived from 'presbyter'. The encyclical *Mediator Dei* sedulously avoids using the corresponding expression.[8] The one really important thing is to understand these things and to uphold the priestly character of the whole Church as a community. There are many things here still to be drawn up into Christian consciousness out of the treasure of revelation.[9]

The new German Catechism of 1955 gives a welcome lead in this way of thinking, with its question: 'What is the Church's holiest duty? The holiest duty of the Church is to celebrate the worship of God.'[10] Worship – that is primarily the Sunday assembly of the faithful as it takes place in thousands upon thousands of places. It is precisely the congregation assembled for worship that demonstrates clearly that we must see the Church in the concrete community made up of earth-bound men and women. The Church that presents the sacrifice is no quasi-personal body, exalted above space and time,[11] but the Church assembled here and now. Although the Church exists as the Church all the time, she only realizes her nature in the fullest sense in the eucharistic assembly of the local congregation. It is here that she becomes 'event'.[12]

To see the Church in her concreteness, to recognize her thus as the Church, is necessary not only from the point of

---

[8] Cf. the relevant passages: *A.A.S.*, xxxix, 1947, pp. 552–8.

[9] G. Söll, 'Das Priestertum der Kirche, ein Desiderat der Ekklesiologie und ihrer Verkündigung' in *Theologie in Geschichte und Gergenwart*, Munich, 1957, pp. 181–98.

[10] *A Catholic Catechism*, London, 1957, p. 23, qu. 100.

[11] At this point we must raise this objection to the otherwise useful source-book by R. Schulte, *Die Messe als Opfer der Kirche. Die Lehre frühmittelalterlicher Autoren über das eucharistische Opfer*, Münster, 1959; cf. also H. B. Meyer in *Zeitschrift für katholische Theologie*, lxxxi, 1959, pp. 489 f.

[12] Karl Rahner, 'Zur Theologie der Pfarre' in *Die Pfarre*, Freiburg, 1956, pp. 27–39, esp. 29 ff. Cf. also H. de Lubac, *The Splendour of the Church*, pp. 104–7.

view of her priesthood. It is necessary if we are not to
allow the dream of an ideal Church to distract us from the
real tasks our Lord set for the institution which was to
occupy the period between his ascension and his second
coming. It is not only in its faithful that the Church is a
field interspersed with weeds: in its official pastoral action
too, not only the Spirit of God but the limitation and
fallibility of weak men also are at work.[13] In this way the
ideal image of the Church acquires more realistic features.
The Church is indeed the bride of Christ, holy and immaculate, without spot or wrinkle (Eph. 5. 27); but she is all
of these things only in her institution, her sacraments, her
faith, and in her holy law.[14] These heavenly endowments
are bestowed upon a Church that is composed of sinful
men, pilgrims trudging along the dusty road of this earth.
Even the leaders of the Church are a prey to human
wretchedness, always seeking perfection in this world, but
never attaining it. Even so the Church remains the *signum
levatum in nationes*,[15] the miracle of divine grace, the life-
giving mother of the faithful. It is of the utmost importance
that, in spite of all realism, our vision of this fact shall not
become dimmed. There have been several occasions when
this has been so. An expert Church historian affirms that
Luther would never have reached his view of the righteous-
ness of God and of justification by faith 'had he not first
of all lost his faith in the Church as a supernatural reality,
and in the sacramental mediation of the redemption of Christ
in and through the Church.'[16]

---

[13] The common tendency to see only the divine element in the Church, and to
allow errors to exist only in the private sphere of Church life, is another example
of the monophysite tendency which would ignore the human element in the
person of Christ. Cf. Y. Congar, *Christ, Marie and the Church*, London, 1957, pp.
54–68.

[14] Pius XII, *Mystici corporis*: *A.A.S.*, xxxv, 1943, p. 225.

[15] Denzinger, *Enchiridion*, n. 1794 (Is. 11, 12).

[16] W. H. van de Pol. *Das reformatorische Christentum*, Einsiedeln, 1956, p. 391.

XI

Grace

IT IS a striking fact that various symbolic expressions of
Christian doctrine from the early Church period are quite
expansive in their portrayal of the Christ-mystery; but what
we call grace is scarcely mentioned. Tertullian, for example,
summarizes the *regula fidei,* and, having spoken of our Lord's
passion, resurrection, and ascension, simply adds: *misisse*
(eum) vicariam vim Spiritus Sancti qui credentes agat, and then
mentions the second coming and eternal life.[1] On a second
occasion he only mentions the resurrection of the body:
venturum iudicare vivos et mortuos per carnis etiam resur-
rectionem.[2] Much the same thing is done by the Council of
Nicaea, which limits itself to the expression: καὶ εἰς τὸ
ἅγιον πνεῦμα.

All this expresses the thought that for those who believe
in God and in Christ the Redeemer, everything else is
almost self-evident – grace, the Church, the sacraments,
eternal glory, and an explicit confession of faith in these
treasures of salvation is not absolutely necessary. We might
very well affirm that the reflex knowledge of how Christ's
redemption is realized in the individual and in mankind at
large is of secondary importance to the simple believer. If
the Christian is quite clear that he must be joined to Christ –
as his name implies—and if, led by the Church, he has found
this link and holds it fast, then light and life have entered
his soul, the Holy Spirit dwells in him, and he possesses the
pledge of eternal blessedness. Efforts of catechists to give

[1] Tertullian, *De praescriptione haer.,* c. 13.
[2] Tertullian, *De virginibus velandis,* c. 1.

children a more precise concept of grace are thus of little importance, at least if some idea is there of the good news of Christ and his work. This is not to say that it is entirely superfluous to speak in detail about grace and the sacraments. But it is important that these should not be discussed in an inappropriate manner. There is a temptation to do this if the isolating analyses and abstract distinctions of the theologians are transferred to catechesis.

For a long time theological discussion about grace in the West was directed predominantly to the process of justification and the possibility of meritorious works. Man's actions had to open up in a specific way to the influence of the merciful God. And so grace was regarded primarily in its relation to moral action. Transference to catechesis and to elementary thinking in general resulted inevitably in grace being understood simply as the requirement for irreproachable acts. The sequence which held sway in the catechisms until very recently – faith, commandments, means of grace – was bound to encourage a moralistic view of the life of grace that threatened to depress this life of grace to the level of the natural order. The concept of the supernatural – current amongst theologians only after the thirteenth century – could do little to help, to say nothing of the abstractness of such a concept.

Some notion of the subject could be much more easily gained by proceeding from habitual grace and the biblical parables which allude to it, or from statements about sonship of God, and our being the temple of God. Amongst spiritual writers it was the French school of Cardinal Bérulle who led the way by placing the idea of the indwelling of the Holy Spirit in the foreground, following the Greek Fathers, and Scheeben restored the idea to its rightful place in theology. But here again an obstacle has to be got out of the way: grace appears within the whole world of faith, as an isolated requirement, as a remarkable, enigmatic pre-condition of divine acceptance, as a purely objective character of the soul, a value that one must *possess*. Copious chapters have been written on the 'glories of divine grace,' none of which mentions any relationship to Christ. Scientific theology itself is now on its guard against such isolation. Karl Rahner affirms: 'There are whole tracts "De gratia Christi" in which for all practical purposes, and seen as a whole, the word "Christus" appears only in the title. These tracts simply presuppose as self-evident, or mention only briefly, that this grace is "merited" precisely by Christ himself. The word "Church" just does not appear at all in these treatises.'[3] He continues: 'And yet we only have a Christian understanding of grace when it is conceived of not only in the most metaphysical way possible, as a divinization, but rather as an assimilation to Christ. And the existential transposition of this is the following of Christ . . .'[4]

And so, in our attempt to make grace meaningful to the Christian mind, we are thrown back upon these thoughts: we must view it as participation in the divine life that Christ has brought into the world. Our exhortation to the faithful will not run: You must *possess* sanctifying grace: but: We must hold fast to our attachment to Christ in faith and love. There are certain liturgical usages, too, which point us along this road. In the Easter Vigil the paschal candle is blessed as a symbol of the risen Christ, and, having been lit, is represented as the source of light for the whole Church; finally it is immersed in the baptismal water, symbolically giving to this also the power to illuminate. All this is an excellent instruction on grace as participation in the Lord's life. When, after baptism, a lighted candle is placed in the child's hand, and a white baptismal cloth laid upon him,

[3] Karl Rahner, *Theological Investigations*, II, p. 113.
[4] Rahner, *op. cit.*, I, p. 199.

this is but the extension of the same eloquent symbolism.

The anointing with Chrism, which in the baptismal liturgy immediately follows the act of baptism, points in the same direction. This was being practised in Rome as early as the third century. 'By this *unctio* the baptized Christian became the Lord's anointed, by it he was incorporated in the royal and priestly race of the New Covenant.'[5] In other words, the effect of baptism as the grace of Christ is described as participation in his holiness.

Having orientated our understanding of the state of grace upon the central point of revelation, it follows that grace signifies a relationship to the mystery of the Trinity on the one hand, and to the Church on the other.[6] Obviously, if grace means participation in the life of Christ, it is also participation in the love of the heavenly Father, which, in the Holy Spirit, embraces not only the well-beloved Son, but all who are incorporated in the mystical body. Grace, then, is also participation in a life through which the holy Church, as the communion of saints, is holy. Thus we see how closely grace and love belong together.

Public worship, too, in this way appears in a new light. The belonging to Christ that is established in grace, more precisely defined through the *character sacramentalis* given in baptism and confirmation as a belonging to Christ the High Priest, is that through which we have *access to the Father,* that is the possibility of approaching God with confidence, and of offering him worthy service in the community of the Church. Grace includes the ability of offer worship: God the Father allows mankind to approach his throne. It is quite plain that these are completely biblical ideas. Even the parable of the wedding-feast belongs in this

[5] H. Elfers, *Die Kirchenordnung Hippolyts von Rom*, Paderborn, 1938, p. 153.

[6] J. Loosen, 'Ekklesiologische, christologische, und trinitatstheologische Elemente im Gnadenbegriff' in *Theologie in Geschichte und Gegenwart*, Munich, 1957, pp. 89–102.

context, not simply on account of the wedding-garment, but also on account of the call, the gracious invitation given by the head of the family. This is precisely the point where we are warned against thinking of our relationship to God in grace and even in the *visio beatifica* as a purely objective relationship – a mere *looking* as at any object. God, who is personal in the most complete sense, is certainly not an object which man confronts merely as knowing subject, and which he can approach as he feels inclined, as he would an impersonal thing. We are invited to approach God through the word that has come to us in Christ. We find the nearness of God not in the heightened acuteness of sight and knowledge, as Greek philosophy implies, but in humble listening, in response to God's gracious call.[7] When viewed from this angle it becomes clear that the nature and vastness of grace are not to be exhausted by the concept of grace as a self-contained distinguishing mark of the soul – and the expression 'sanctifying grace', derived from scientific analysis, is frequently misunderstood along these lines; we are concerned rather with a personal relationship to a personal God who has offered us his love and friendship in Christ.

From the fact that in grace the personal God draws man as a personal being to himself and receives him as a friend, it follows that grace is no inflexible entity, but ought to be kept in association with its corresponding action. The structure of the new German Catechism of 1955 was well conceived, therefore. The section on baptism as the source

[7] Cf. A. Brunner, 'Gott schauen' in *Zeitschrift für katholische Theologie*, LXXIII, 1951, pp. 214–22. Brunner points out that the pertinent biblical parables: feast, marriage, sonship, co-citizenship, 'are all derived from the sphere of personal relations between men, in which vision does essentially play a part, but remains an element secondary to personal intercourse through communication, sharing the same views, loving co-existence' (p. 218). 'A person lets himself be known only by freely revealing himself' (p. 219). (Reprinted in A. Brunner, *Vom christlichen Liebe*, Würzburg, 1962.)

of new life contains the doctrine of grace; this section is immediately followed by further sections of instruction on the theological virtues in which the life of grace must unfold. At this place, therefore, the catechism speaks of faith, hope, and charity, and then also of the imitation of Christ and of prayer as the tangible verification of these virtues.

In following this line of thought we do not intend to contest the fact that faith is primarily an assent to truth. Nevertheless in practical instruction it is bound to do good if we do not so much stress the pure clarifying of concepts as try to see faith as the surrender of the whole man to God who reveals himself. The word 'believe' is, in fact, etymologically connected with 'love'. Not for nothing did Augustine bring out the linguistic peculiarity of our Creed, pointing out that we do not simply believe God, but believe *in* God, thus already including the impulse of hope and love in faith.[8] Faith is concerned with more than mere objects which one calmly affirms; it also denotes an attitude in which man responds to God and the offer of his love.[9]

The same more personalist view and mode of speech is in place also when we are speaking of the sacraments. The older sort of catechisms gather the sacraments under the title 'means of grace.' They are undoubtedly means of grace in a certain sense, although we must steer clear of the notion that they are put at our disposal so that we may, by these means, create grace at will. They are means in the hands of Christ who desires to enrich us, rather than means in our possession. It is Christ who acts in the sacraments. It is he who has bridged the distance in space and time that

[8] There is no significance in the fact that initially this has to do merely with a peculiarity of Church Latin. Christine Mohrmann, *Etudes sur le latin des chrétiens*, Rome, 1958, pp. 195–203: *Credere in*.

[9] This is the notion of the *fides qua creditur* (in contrast to exclusive concentration upon the content of faith). Fr. X. Arnold has drawn attention to this in several writings, notably in *Dienst am Glauben*, Freiburg, 1948, p. 24 etc.

separates us from his death and resurrection. For this reason the Fathers saw him at work in the sacraments,[10] and the German Catechism of 1955 has returned to the same manner of expression. For example, the question about the effects of baptism is not phrased: 'What does Baptism effect?' but 'What does Christ bring about in Baptism?' By this form of presentation we guard against conceiving the sacraments more or less consciously as a species of magic, and ensure that the sacraments are seen as fitted into that encounter between God and man which has its beginning and foundation in the coming of Christ.[11]

[10] Cf. the famous saying of Augustine, *in Joh. tract.* 6, 7 (*P. L.* xxxv, 1428): *Ipse est qui baptizat*. Similarly Chrysostom, *In 2 Tim. hom.* 2, 4 (*P. G.* LXII, 612) with reference to the Eucharist.

[11] O. Semmelroth, *Gott und Mensch in Begegnung*, Frankfurt, 1956; E. H. Schillebeeckx, *Christ: The Sacrament of Encounter with God*, London, 1963.

XII

The Eucharist

OUR MEETING with Christ is most intense in the Eucharist. Until not many years ago it was quite common to find presentations of the doctrine of the Eucharist which spoke first of all about the sacrament, then about communion, and finally about the sacrifice of the Mass. The cathechisms often completely separated the doctrine of the sacrifice of the Mass from the rest of the doctrine of the Eucharist, and placed it, say, under the heading of the third commandment of God or the precepts of the Church. Christian piety was in line with this: communion, Mass, adoration of the Blessed Sacrament, were three separate spheres of devotional practice.

It is important, therefore, that now the Eucharist, for all its complexity, should once again be seen chiefly in its primary and true function, from which all else is derived. It is not primarily an object for our adoration, nor yet for the nourishment of the soul, but is, as its name indicates, a sacrifice of thanksgiving, of sacrifice within the assembled congregation. It is only this basic view that gathers all of the aspects into a unity.

Our Lord himself presented the sacrament to his apostles with a prayer of thanksgiving (εὐχαριστήσας), and the entire tradition in every rite of East and West knows the Eucharist primarily and only as the celebration of public worship of God, for which the faithful assemble, particularly on Sunday. In the first century the *Didache* stresses this meeting on the Lord's Day: κατὰ κυριακὴν δὲ κυριου; half a century later Justin stresses the same thing – on the

day named after the sun. Sunday is called the Lord's Day –
κυριακή, *dominica* – because on this day the Lord as κύριος
crowned the work of our redemption with his resurrection,
and revealed the new life in which we are to have a share.
Hence it is on this day that the commemoration of the
redemption must be celebrated, as our Lord had ordained
when he said: 'Do this for a memorial of me.'

This leads us to take note of another important feature
of the eucharistic mystery: the celebration of the Eucharist
is a sacrifice, it is true – the sacrifice of the New Covenant,
but first of all it is a memorial. It is the memorial celebration
of the redeeming Passion in the same way as Sunday is the
memorial day of the perfected work of redemption. From the
start Eucharist and Sunday have belonged together. Thinking of the Mass almost exclusively as a sacrifice is a one-
sided attitude resulting from the doctrinal controversies of
the sixteenth century. The sacrificial aspect of the Mass was
contested, the threatened point defended and to some extent
built up into an impregnable fortress. Account was now
taken of the memorial aspect only in so far as the correlative
sacrifice was mentioned, the relationship which pointed
back to the sacrifice upon the cross. The period leading up
to our own has been accustomed to speak with equal
emphasis of the *memoria passionis* – the Canon of the Mass
has always expressed this thought: *Unde et memores . . .
offerimus.* Thus although the Middle Ages spoke much of the
sacrifice and the fruits of the sacrifice, the memorial character
of the Mass was still much to the fore, even in the popular
imagination. This is shown by the allegorical interpretation
which regarded the Mass as a play in which – admittedly
in a thoroughly external fashion[1] – salvation-history, and
the passion of our Lord in particular, were portrayed. In the

---

[1]Cf. A. Kolping, 'Amalar von Metz und Florus von Lyon' in *Zeitschrift für katholische Theologie*, LXXIII, 1951, pp. 424–64.

Corpus Christi procession at the start of the modern period
the passion of Christ, illustrated by its prototypes, still
forms the central motif of the glorification of the Blessed
Sacrament.[2]

The memorial certainly is not meant to be restricted to the
passion of Christ. What does the Canon say? – *memores . . .
tam beatae passionis, necnon et ab inferis resurrectionis, sed et in
coelos gloriosae ascensionis.* Only thus do we achieve consonance
with the memorial character of Sunday – a consonance that
was there from the very start. Sunday and the Mass must
both, in equal measure, be coloured by the basic tone of
Easter. This means too that it is necessary once again to
bring out more clearly the true meaning of Sunday.

To restore its religious importance to our all too secular
Sunday it is not enough merely to tighten up the precept of
the Church in every way possible; it can be achieved only
by making the religious content of Sunday come fully alive
once more. Sunday is more than simply the day upon which
we honour God. It is the day upon which Christ, the first
of the new creation, rose up from the darkness of death.
Hence it is the day upon which the Christian ought to be
deeply conscious of the treasure which has come to him in
Christ and the Church, the day upon which, along with the
whole congregation, he gives thanks to God, with holy
joy. For this reason the Christian mind has for centuries
counted Sunday not as the seventh day of the Old Testament,
but as the eighth day, the day upon which the Creator
continued the work of the seven days and completed it in
Christ: it was regarded as the Christian conclusion and
climax of the week.[3] Thus the number eight has come to be
the symbol of the perfection of the new life – so much so

---

[2] A. Dörrer, *Tiroler Umgangsspiele*, Innsbruck, 1957, pp. 239 ff.

[3] Jungmann, *Gewordene Liturgie*, Innsbruck, 1941, pp. 217–21. The races that were
not converted until the Middle Ages – Slavs, Hungarians, Baltic peoples – used
names for the days of the week, beginning the count with Monday.

that baptismal chapels, in which this new life is transmitted, were almost always built upon an octagonal plan.

Friday of the Passion (and Wednesday of the betrayal), as preparation, then became related to the Sunday of the Resurrection. It seemed obvious to people that Friday ought to be observed as a fast-day in preparation for the joy of Sunday. The weekly cycle then was – and should again become – a constantly recurring pointer to the basic facts of our Christian life, and should lead us towards the corporate, solemn celebration of the Eucharist on Sunday, just as, on the larger scale, the Christian Year is a leading up to Easter. This harmony between Sunday and the celebration of the Eucharist ought to be fostered also by the shape of the Sunday Mass. The prayer of thanksgiving should be a real expression of the things for which we do give holy thanks – as we find in many ancient Sunday Prefaces of the Carolingian sacramentaries. As soon as thoughts are turned into the language of prayer they must appear primarily as thanksgiving.[4] It is obvious that in God's eyes thanksgiving is at the same time adoration and obeisance.[5] It is not by chance that the eucharistic prayer always runs into the *Sanctus*, which joins the congregation upon earth in a unity of adoration with the celestial choirs.

Sacrifice thus signifies but a further step in the same ascent: it is the sacrifice of Christ, but at the same time the sacrifice of the Church, offered in union with Christ; in distinction to the sacrifice upon the cross, it is primarily the sacrifice of the Church. Since the Council of Trent the understanding of the sacrifice of the Mass has often been obstructed by the apologetic tendency to overstrain its

---

[4] We should note the etymological connection between 'think' and 'thank', just as εὐχαριστεῖν means nothing other than to admit that one has been highly gifted – εὐχάριστος.

[5] The appropriate basic biblical language alternates, as we know, between the thought of thanking and praising. This applies to the Hebrew *barach* and to some extent also to the Greek εὐχαριστεῖν.

identity with the sacrifice of the cross, and to see in it nothing except the one re-presented sacrifice upon the cross, the sacrifice which Christ renews here and now, but in an unbloody manner. This way of thinking provides scarcely any bridge to the actual shape of the liturgy of the Mass. In reality, from its very beginning the structure of the Mass portrays it as *our sacrifice*; it is our entering into the sacrifice of Christ; it is our affiliation with his oblation to the heavenly Father – so much so, that the symbols of his oblation, the offerings of his body and blood, are allowed to represent our offering also. The Mass is thus the great mountain-top which our poor efforts are for ever being challenged to ascend; it is, at the same time, grace made tangible, raising us up to the stature of our Lord and Master.

Today we are very properly recommended day by day to lay our every action in the hands of God. We are all familiar with set forms of Morning Offering.[6] Most of the texts for this offering are addressed to the Sacred Heart, but it is still perfectly clear that such an offering is intended to bear some relation to the sacrifice of the Mass. Ought we not to acknowledge that the holy Mass itself is much more powerful than any other formula, is indeed the specific and true expression of this self-oblation? In fact, this recurrent total self-oblation is the true meaning and purpose of participation in the holy sacrifice. By this participation we are merely fulfilling the law which St Peter prescribed for Christians (1 Pet. 2. 4 f.): they are to join themselves to Christ, the living corner-stone, and build themselves up into a holy priesthood 'to offer spiritual sacrifices acceptable to God through Jesus Christ.' This clearly refers to two things: our exterior actions, and also the summing up of all these actions in the Eucharist.

---

[6] The Apostolic Penitentiary allows for this to be said *quavis formula* and endows it with a plenary indulgence: *A.A.S.*, LIII, 1961, p. 827.

Sermons and edifying literature of the declining Middle Ages followed the wrong track of regarding the Mass chiefly from the point of view of the benefits which it conferred upon those who took part in it. In this way the calculation of the *fructus Missae* became one of the most important topics of eucharistic theology, a topic which, having degenerated further, led ultimately in the popular mind to that rank overgrowth against which the Reformers inveighed with such passion.[7] It is perfectly true that the celebration of the Eucharist brings down blessings upon us; for this reason we call it *missa*, i.e. the dismissal-blessing; it is true that it sanctifies our souls *ex opere operato*; but consideration of these benefits ought not to dominate education concerning the Mass. The primary function of the celebration of the Eucharist is not, as it is with the other sacraments, to produce benefits for us, but to glorify God. Even spiritual advantage is not the prime objective of the Mass. At all events this is the view we find in the primitive Church. A recent monograph on the eucharistic doctrine of St John Chrysostom – the *doctor Eucharistiae* – proves most instructively that Chrysostom 'does not educate through the Eucharist, but for the Eucharist.'[8] This is undoubtedly the noblest and most all-embracing function of Christian education: to educate people for the Mass; for this means education that leads to resonance with the beat of the Sacred Heart of Jesus and to union of life with Christ in whom God is glorified. When our lives have thus found sure anchorage in God, and Sunday by Sunday or even daily we find God anew in the Mass, despite all the world's distractions, spiritual fruit comes all unsought.

[7] A. Franz, *Die Messe im deutschen Mittelalter*, Freiburg, 1902, pp. 36–72; cf. E. Iserloh, 'Der Wert der Messe in der Diskussion der Theologen vom Mittelalter bis zum 16. Jahrhundert' in *Zeitschrift für katholische Theologie*, LXXXIII, 1961, pp. 44–79.
[8] G. Fittkau, *Der Begriff des Mysteriums bei Joh. Chrysostomus*, Bonn, 1953, p. 129.

'Genuine public worship is a benefit, a restorative for man, in his external needs and in the deepest spiritual needs of his heart; genuine worship is a sanatorium for all ills, error, and blindness, a rampart around the individual and the congregation.'[9]

Exclusive stress upon the sacrifice of Christ, and unrestricted identification of the Mass with the sacrifice of Calvary, along with the ignoring of what we, as the Church, have to seek to do on our part, leads us away from the true liturgy of the Mass in yet another respect. Christ's sacrifice upon the cross was the sacrifice that redeemed the world. In its essence it was primarily a sacrifice of atonement, the self-immolation of the Lord as the *ransom-price for many* (Matt. 20. 18). The blood that then flowed *for the forgiveness of sins* becomes, in the Church, the purifying bath of baptism; in the sacrament of penance it sprinkles the soul of the sinner.

The Eucharist, however, is primarily designed for those who have already been purified in Christ's blood and enjoy his new life. The sacrifice of the Mass is not the sacrifice for the redemption of the world, but the sacrifice made by the redeemed. In it we do indeed find the same sacrificing priest, the same gifts offered; but the *manner of offering* is not the same.[10] Now the High Priest no longer makes the sacrifice on his own, as on the cross. Making present his sacrifice upon the cross, he gathers his Church about him in order to offer the *sacrificium laudis* along with them. This is the pure offering made in every place, of which the prophet Malachy spoke. For this very reason the sacrifice of the Mass is εὐχαριστία; and it takes this form in every

---

[9] H. Volk, 'Theologische Besinnung über die Feier der Sonntagsmesse' in *Eucharistiefeier am Sonntag*, ed. J. Wagner and D. Zahringer, Trier, 1951, p. 52.

[10] Council of Trent, Session XXII, c. 2 Denzinger, n. 940): *sola offerendi ratione diversa*. The difference in *ratio* clearly means more than that the exterior rite is different, that it is unbloody. A new purpose now lies behind the offering.

Christian liturgy. Εὐχαριστῶμεν τῷ κυρίω is the call addressed to the congregation. The Mass is also an atoning sacrifice, it is true; it can be offered for the living and for the dead, as Trent emphasizes.[11] Indeed the idea of atonement and of forgiveness of sins in virtue of the sacrifice is incorporated in every Mass;[12] but it does not sound the underlying note of the Mass and does not govern its structure. The sacrifice of praise and the sacrifice of atonement are not on the same plane.

The Mass is designed as the Church's sacrifice of praise and thanksgiving. Ever since the fresh realization of the Church as the *plebs sancta* gathered round the priest as instrument of the High Priest, the liturgical movement has been at work bringing the active participation of the *plebs sancta* into its own. This movement is well advanced in many parts of Europe, although its forms of expression may be temporary and very much the product of their times. Church architecture and furnishing have been profoundly affected. The view of the Mass as purely Christ's sacrifice and the fountain of blessing derived therefrom, and the resultant notion of 'assisting at' Mass or 'hearing Mass devoutly,' had led not only to the construction of many side-altars in churches, but to the placing of as many of these as possible in view of the congregation, so that they could assist at several Masses simultaneously. Today in the church that is constructed logically for the corporate celebration of Mass by the whole congregation, the side-altars disappear and the church is built as a unified space where all eyes are directed to the one altar upon which the sacrifice is corporately offered, the one meal prepared for all.

[11] *Ibid.*
[12] In the *Hanc igitur*: *ab aeterna damnatione nos eripi*; in the *Memento* of the dead; and in the *Nobis quoque peccatoribus*.

In German-speaking countries about 1930 a unique process took place with the gradual maturing of the liturgical movement. The communion of the faithful which, even after Pius X's time, continued in isolation, became recognized everywhere almost simultaneously as a sacrificial meal, and then whenever possible became integrated in the Mass, without any direction from above.[13]

Automatically a new attitude to the reception of the Blessed Sacrament gradually emerged. The dominant idea ceased to be that of the visit, which had characterized the communion-prayers in many prayer-books, and became that of the sacred meal in which one shared at the *mensa coelestis* – an idea presupposed and upheld throughout the whole liturgy. Only along such lines of greater (perhaps too great) breadth could the frequent communion movement of Pius X keep going. Holy communion is the more or less obvious confirmation of, and seal upon, participation in the holy sacrifice. It is no longer the blink of light that marks off certain points in the year or the month from an everyday life that has been given over to the world;[14] now it is the brightness of the whole of Christian life which has become more clearly aware of closeness to God. Nothing is lost by our realization that this nearness of God, which we call the life of grace, consists in Christ's dwelling within our hearts,[15] and that this indwelling, which medieval theology described as spiritual communion,[16] is in the end even

---

[13] For a more detailed description of this process with reference to catechesis see Henry Fischer, *Eucharistie-katechese und liturgische Erneuerung*, Düsseldorf, 1959.

[14] The spiritual rule of life prescribed by St Catherine of Siena for a rich citizen of Siena has exerted a profound effect right down to the present day. She prescribed: daily Mass (and Little Office of our Lady), monthly confession, communion on great feast-days or at least once a year. Cited without source by C. Butler, *Wege christlichen Lebens,* Einsiedeln, 1944, p. 127.

[15] Eph. 3. 17. Cf. G. Söhngen, 'Christi Gegenwart in uns durch Glauben' in *Die Messe in der Glaubensverkündigung,* 2nd ed., Freiburg, 1953, pp. 24–8.

[16] H. R. Schlette, *Kommunikation und Sakrament (Quaestiones disputatae* VIII), Freiburg, 1960; *id., Die Lehre von der geistlichen Kommunion bei Bonaventura, Albert d. Gr., und Thomas von Aquin,* Munich, 1958. This spiritual communion is not, however, the

more important than sacramental communion.[17] If we are to advance in the spiritual life we must see clearly that permanent union with Christ can and must be strengthened in many different ways, and that the *opus operatum* of holy communion must not in any event be allowed to stand in isolation, as though in itself providing an infalliable, more or less magically effective means of spiritual progress. For this reason one should maintain a certain detachment even towards daily communion.[18]

Long before communion had come to be separated from the celebration of the Eucharist,[19] another separation had been effected: the Blessed Sacrament had been isolated as an object of veneration. It had always been accepted as self-evident that the Blessed Sacrament should be treated with great reverence, and be reserved in a seemly fashion. But for a very long time no one thought of developing any special cult in its honour. To this day the Eastern rites know of no such cult. Some astonishment was aroused when it was shown that special veneration of the Eucharist played no part in the devotional life of either Gregory the Great or St Bernard.[20] Soon after St Bernard's time, however, there appeared that surge of eucharistic devotion, mentioned above,[21] which required, to begin with, that the Blessed Sacrament be gazed upon in awe, and then that it be

same as the mental communion which consists in a longing for sacramental communion, a pious practice that has real significance only in exceptional cases in the normal circumstances of worship in an age of daily communion.

[17] Karl Rahner, *Theological Investigations* II, pp. 109–33: 'Personal and Sacramental Piety'.

[18] It is in harmony with this attitude if a priest, when travelling, prefers to forgo celebrating Mass (and if necessary forgo receiving communion) rather than upset the routine of a whole convent in the late forenoon.

[19] This happened first of all in modern times, and became a fixed arrangement only after the turn of the eighteenth-nineteenth century. Cf. P. Browe, 'Wann fing man an, die Kommunion ausserhalb der Messe auszuteilen?' in *Theologie und Glaube*, XXIII, 1931, pp. 755–62.

[20] C. Butler, *Wege der christlichen Lebens*, 1944, pp. 79 f.

[21] Cf. p. 43.

revered in various ways. With the construction of the tabernacle, which since the sixteenth or seventeenth century
has been part of the furniture of every major church,
veneration of the Blessed Sacrament received powerful
encouragement: the Blessed Sacrament moved to the central point in the house of God, and thus arose what we call
tabernacle-devotion, a type of piety which, from the standpoint of Catholic dogma, is legitimate and justified at all
times, but which, in the circumstances of impeded communion such as we have mentioned, was also called upon
to fill a gap. There can be no doubt that in the course of
centuries much fruit has been produced out of this devotion, and still is being produced; through it, indeed, the
peak of religious life has sometimes been reached.

Nevertheless this style of devotion frequently assumes
remarkable forms. A church would seem to become the
house of God for a number of Christians only if the eternal
light burns there before the tabernacle.[22] Again, we hear
talk of a special life which Jesus lives in the tabernacle, and
questions about what senses he might require there.[23]
We even hear people expressing pity for the silent recluse
in his endless solitude. It is quite obvious that such meditations, which were still nourishing eucharistic devotion at
the beginning of this century,[24] are not so appropriate today when people have become more acutely aware of the
fact that our Lord presents his body to us in his sacrament
chiefly to be offered and received.

And yet no one doubts that it is most reasonable to grant

[22] Even in the reformed rite for the consecration of a church of 1962 the exposition of the sacramental presence forms no element of the sanctification of the
building.
[23] Cf. the speculations of Cardinal A. de Cienfuegos (d. 1739). See H. Dutouquet,
'Cienfuegos' in *Dictionnaire de Théologie Catholique*, II, pp. 2511 f.; A. Michel, 'La
Messe', *ibid.*, x, pp. 1189 f.
[24] The simple poems of the convert Cordula Peregrina: *Was das ewige Licht
erzählt*, first published in 1885, a year later than the Missal of Anselm Schott, had
run to twenty-two editions by 1922 – the same number as Schott's Missal.

a prominent place within the church to the Blessed Sacrament which the Church possesses and which must be reserved outside the celebration of Mass, at least for the benefit of the sick, and to venerate it in this place. If the Postcommunion of the Mass for the consecration of a church sees in the material structure an allusion to the spiritual edifice of holy Church which has been built of 'living and chosen stones' to the glory of God, we have only to hold fast to this same imagery to see that the tabernacle, even more than the altar, symbolizes the chief corner-stone upon which the whole building is raised (cf. Eph. 2. 20 ff.). We enter the house of God and know ourselves to be once more welcomed into the holy congregation whose Head is Christ. Even without meaning primarily to visit the Blessed Sacrament, a visit to the church does join us once again more closely to the world of God.

All this makes it plain that to find the proper placing for the tabernacle: more precisely, to find its proper accommodation to the necessity of clearly giving the altar its central place as the site of the corporately celebrated sacrifice, is an almost insoluble problem for the modern architect. Strictly speaking, the problem has only existed since 1918, when, at the very moment the liturgical movement was leading a return to the original emphases in eucharistic devotion, the *Codex Juris Canonici* in *can.* 1268 summed up the consequences of the eucharistic devotion of a previous age by saying that the Blessed Sacrament should be reserved *in praecellentissimo ac nobilissimo ecclesiae loco ac proinde regulariter in altari maiore*, in a tabernacle placed, indeed, at the centre of the altar. The Roman *Rituale* of 1614 – not binding upon the whole Church – had prescribed a tabernacle, but had not specified at which altar.[25] The provincial

---

[25] *Rituale Romanum*, V, 1, 6. The relevant text remains unaltered in the new edition of 1952.

Council of Cologne in 1860 still allowed the 'sacrament-house' as an equally legitimate solution. As the *Codex* specified the high altar only as the standard case, since then architects have evolved solutions in which a special Blessed Sacrament altar or a tabernacle structure is provided in the main axis of the church, either in front of the high altar at the entrance to the choir, or behind it in the apse.[26] After Pius XII had remarked that we are concerned not so much with the physical presence of the tabernacle upon the altar as with the prevention of any disrespect to the eucharistic presence,[27] the Congregation of Rites issued the limiting regulation that in churches with only one altar, the tabernacle must always be erected upon this altar.[28]

From the very start, therefore, the possibilities are severely limited. Considerations of convenience, which with more frequent communions after the Council of Trent led to the predominance of the altar-tabernacle, will probably govern most solutions today also. In large churches and cathedrals, and in churches where the Divine Office is sung, the law allows of exceptions – welcomes them, indeed. In these cases, besides the desire not to cause disturbance, the older tradition must also have played its part; for by itself the Divine Office could scarcely have required a separation of altar and tabernacle. Moreover, special indulgences were attached to the recitation of the Breviary before the Blessed Sacrament.[29] We must see the tabernacle as a hindrance more to the celebration of Mass than to the recitation of the Office, because the presence of the Blessed

[26] H. v. Meurers, 'Altar und Tabernakel' in *Liturgisches Jahrbuch*, III, 1953, pp. 10–28.
[27] Address to members of the Pastoral Liturgical Congress of Assisi on 22 Sept. 1956. Cf. J. Wagner, *Erneuerung der Liturgie aus dem Geiste der Seelsorge*, Trier, 1957, pp. 358 f.
[28] 1 June 1957. Cf. *Liturgisches Jahrbuch*, VII, 1957, p. 251.
[29] Several decrees since 1930: *Enchiridion Indulgentiarum*, Rome, 1950, n. 371, 736, 758.

Eucharist from the very start of the Mass must prejudice the logic of the course of the celebration. The liturgy of the Mass, apart from the genuflexion at the beginning and the end, pays no attention at all to the Blessed Sacrament locked within the tabernacle upon the altar. We may assume, therefore, that as the ideas behind the liturgical movement become increasingly respectable, ecclesiastical legislation, which in so many cases has measured forms of eucharistic devotion against the standard of preserved tradition,[30] will recognize the interest of modern church-building in a free-standing, unencumbered altar, and will open the way, in this case too, to solutions in the spirit of tradition.

Just as no one would dream of abolishing the feast of Corpus Christi, neither will the adoration of the Blessed Sacrament as a special cult, or as a blessing at the end of some other act of worship, ever lose its rightful place.

There is a problem that we might do well to reflect upon at this point. Is it appropriate, in a devotion that is held before the Blessed Sacrament exposed, to address prayer to the Saviour here present? It is significant that this does not happen, for example, in those prayers which we say as we bow over the sacred Host immediately before communion; and yet these are explicitly directed to Christ. The petition runs: *Domine Jesu Christe . . . libera me per hoc sacrosanctum corpus et sanguinem tuum*. In this prayer from the ninth century the thought is still alive that the true and only mode of Christ's existence is that which he lives *in gloria Dei Patris*. It is this presence that appears like a focus, and becomes sacramentally efficacious at a thousand places in the Blessed Sacrament. Conversely, however, the Blessed Sacrament is intended to remain in some degree transparent

---

[30] Cf. Rome's attitude towards exposition of the Blessed Sacrament. In contrast to the practice in northern countries, Rome provides for few cases. – *Codex Juris Can., can.* 1274

so that we look through it towards the one glorified life of our Lord as he 'lives and reigns with the Father in the unity of the Holy Spirit.' It is the life of the Transfiguration which, in another mode, shines in the hearts of Christians as the life of grace, as a pneumatic presence, enabling us to pray, live and act, 'in Christ.' An Italian theologian appropriately remarks: 'The consciousness amongst his people of Christ's presence as Mediator, so lively during the first centuries, may be the justification for the fact that for several centuries no explicit cult of the Blessed Sacrament appeared outside the framework of the liturgy.'[31] This is not to deny that such a cult would be reconcilable with that newly aroused consciousness.

What has been said is intended merely to point to the principle: the specific purpose of the sacrament is not the cult, but the celebration of the Eucharist, primarily its Sunday celebration by the assembled congregation. In this sense the Eucharist is the climax, the summit, of all pastoral care. When one has succeeded in leading a congregation in its various classes, groups, and ages, to a point from which they can see the corporate and worthy celebration of the Sunday Mass as the true expression of their Christian life, pastoral care has achieved its purpose: it has performed what was once the vocation of the precursor: *parare Domino plebem perfectam*.

We are accustomed to list the Eucharist as the third of the sacraments. This corresponds to its role within the scheme of initiation-sacraments at the beginning of the Christian life: baptism, confirmation, Eucharist. The addition thereafter of the other four sacraments somewhat obscures the unique position of the Eucharist in the scheme. But the other four are appended as a kind of supplement, a second

---

[31] P. Dacquino, 'La formula paolina "in Cristo Gesu"' in *Scuola Cattolica*, LXXXVII, 1959, p. 284, note 26.

line of pious practices in which the generic concept of a sacrament is likewise realized. In reality, like baptism and confirmation, although in a different way, they form the foundation for the possibility of the Eucharist: they purify the people of God from sin, they extend the priestly powers, they bless the exit from Christian life, and sanctify the door through which new generations press into the Church to become the host who glorify God in the Eucharist.[32]

And so, for several decades now, the correct manner of celebrating the Eucharist, or more precisely, to achieve the correct manner of the participation of the faithful in the Eucharist, has very properly been accounted the most pressing task in pastoral work. Since the appearance in Germany in 1942 of the *Guiding Principles of the Liturgical Form of Parish Worship* many countries and many separate dioceses have published their own directories concerning the corporate celebration of holy Mass. Finally, on 3 September 1958, Rome itself published the celebrated *Instruction*. The chief problem was to reach a lively corporate celebration of the Mass despite the unfamiliarity of its language. This instruction lays down the rule that there should be a commentator who reproduces briefly the main content of the prayers said aloud at the altar by the celebrant. This follows the French and Italian model. In Germany a different system had been developed and had received approval by Rome.[33] The German method was to have, not a reader, but a precentor or leader of prayer who said aloud simultaneously with the celebrant, but in the vernacular, those official prayers which, preceded by a greeting and invitation, are

[32] Cf. O. Semmelroth, *Vom Sinn der Sakramente*, Frankfurt, 1960, pp. 70 ff. For this reason I intended the sections on the Eucharist in my book *Public Worship* (1957) to be the conclusion and crown of the chapters entitled 'The Sacramental Rites.'

[33] This method also was accepted as regular in terms of the *Instructio* by the Roman arrangement of 23 December 1958.

said silently by the celebrant. Of necessity this method was based upon the Low Mass, which in the 'Prayer-Song-Mass'[34] became clothed with some solemnity and elevated to the status of the Sunday Mass of the congregation. In addition the 'German High Mass', the Mass with hymns in German, offered a possibility, at least in the *missa cantata*, for the congregation to join in the movement of the Mass. This style of participation has frequently been requested and allowed in missionary countries.[35] These represent much-needed solutions for an interim period. It is hoped that the momentum of Vatican II will lead the way to a revision of traditional forms of the celebration of the Eucharist and to a solution that will harmonize the heritage of the past with the insights and requirements of our new age. The working commission entrusted with this work faces an enormous task. There is no lack of concrete promptings and suggestions. The decisive thing will be the effort made, not to reinstate an ideal form of the Eucharist such as may be celebrated by some cathedral chapter or monastery of highly trained monks, but to devise a form in which Christian people can glorify God and rejoice in their faith.[36]

[34] Cf. articles 'Prayer-Song-Mass' and 'German High Mass' in Podhradsky, *A Dictionary of the Liturgy*, London, 1967.

[35] J. Hofinger, J. Kellner, *Liturgische Erneuerung in der Weltmission*, Innsbruck, 1957, p. 199; B. Fischer, 'Deutsches Hochamt, II' in *Lexikon für Theologie und Kirche*, III, 1959, pp. 278 f.

[36] *Constitution on the Sacred Liturgy* (Whitegate Publications, 1963).

XIII

Prayer and the Language of Prayer

FOR THE Catholic Christian the Eucharist is the first and indispensable form in which we honour God through prayer; but it is not the only form. Not only is there the silent prayer of the individual, but there must also be forms of prayerful turning to God, expressed in words, both for the assembled faithful and for the individual. In these too the treasures of faith are mirrored, and every revival of faith's awareness has a stake in these forms of prayer, desiring that here, too, the essential law of Christian prayer be fulfilled. A few thoughts about the relationship between prayer and the message of the faith will not, therefore, be out of place.

In the last analysis true prayer is always an entering into the mind of God; but it does not necessarily consist in preoccupation with the details of divine revelation. Most important of all is that we submerge our unsteady will in the holy will of God, in shame, in repentance, in holy joy, in peace and confidence. Hence prayer, in its deepest essence, is largely independent of words. It does not rely upon a comprehensive knowledge of faith nor upon a clearly arranged intellectual system of faith. Very little theological material is contained in the *Imitation of Christ*, and yet how it is pervaded by the spirit of prayer! And so a true piety is possible, the conceptual foundation of which is far removed from a well-ordered awareness of the faith, and which may well consist in an astonishing variety of devotions, practices, and traditions.[1] The liturgy itself provides an example of

[1] Cf. the series of articles 'Anregungen eines alten Seelsorgers' in the Austrian

how prayer only roughly corresponds to its verbal support,
how, in fact, it can never strictly correspond to it. We have
only to observe the manner in which large stretches of the
Breviary are composed. In the form in which it has come
down to us, a form evolved as the choral prayer of monas-
teries and collegiate churches, it is more concerned – apart
from feast-day offices and its general framework – with
filling up a specific period of time, spent before God, with
sacred words, than with unfolding a well-ordered train of
thought. In creating the order of the psalms in the Breviary,
they simply took the Psalter, began in the first nocturn of
Sunday with Psalm 1, and – until the revision by Pius X –
by the third nocturn of Saturday had reached Psalm 108.
A second series began at Psalm 109 in Sunday Vespers
and went through the rest of the psalms at Vespers on week-
days. The sense of the psalms was not meant to be ignored.
In the Rule of St Benedict we read: *ut mens nostra concordet
voci* (c. 19); but the grammatical text played a very small
part, which is proved also by the fact that in more than a
thousand years no one seems to have been disturbed by the
many incomprehensible passages in the Latin text. In so far
as men were interested in the meaning of the text, it was not
the literal sense which they sought.[2] Indeed, there were
even instructions on prayer which consciously encouraged

Klerusblatt, XCI, 1958, pp. 33–106. The writer, a successful and venerable city pastor,
himself a man of prayer, mentions a number of devotions: to the Holy Name, the
'eucharistic God,' the Sacred Heart, Christ the King, and, above all, the Precious
Blood and the Heart of Mary. He speaks enthusiastically of the dawning epoch of
the Heart of Mary (pp. 97 f.). He advocates the intensive use of ejaculatory prayer.
For him holy water is a 'miraculous means' of calling down God's blessing, and
should be used to sprinkle important letters before posting them. Exorcism should
be widely practised. For him miraculous medals and the brown Carmelite scapular
are important elements in piety and pastoral activity (pp. 105 ff.). We see the same
sort of devotion in P. Lukas Etlin, O.S.B. (d. 1927), well known for his great
charitable welfare-work after the war, and highly revered on account of his piety,
the character of which is shown in the newspaper *Tabernacle and Purgatory* which he
edited. Cf. also *Lexikon für Theologie und Kirche*, III, 1931, p. 895.

[2] Cf. above, p. 23.

the worshipper to ignore the actual text of the prayer.[3] The Oratorian, Louis Thomassin (d. 1695), a great expert on patristic literature, was still advocating the principle: where the will to prayer is present, it can find nourishment even in unintelligible words.[4] This thought may warn us against forming too harsh a judgement upon the use of the Latin Office as observed until recently by many communities of nuns, ignorant of that language. Especially where the will to glorify God is expressed by the singing of the Office, psalmody can be meaningful even with a minimum of understanding of the words. Very often it can be a single word, a half comprehended phrase, which fires the soul with devotion and joy. Joseph Wittig tells us how only a single phrase from his childhood prayerbook remained alive in his memory: 'Jesus, thou King of eternal glory!' He had no idea what 'glory' really meant, but his childish mind imagined a whole fairy-land of happiness and bliss, light and splendour, love and kindness.

Of all the practical reasons put forward for the retention of Latin in the liturgy, the most cogent is that in public worship language does not serve quite the same function as in the everyday intercourse of men. Here it does not serve mutual understanding, but our talking with God[5] – hence the tendency in all religions to retain ancient terms even after they have ceased to be understood. It is said of Julian the Apostate, reviver of Roman paganism, that he addressed his temple priests in this fashion: 'The eternity of the gods is to be honoured in the unchanging form of worship.'[6] At the same time we must supplement this by affirming that

---

[3] S. Hilpisch, *Chorgebet und Frömmigkeit im Spätmittelalter: Heilige Überlieferung*, Münster, 1938, pp. 623–84.
[4] L. Thomassin, *Über das Göttliche Offizium und seine Verbindung mit dem inneren Gebet*, Düsseldorf, 1952, pp. 69 f.
[5] Christine Mohrmann, 'Le latin liturgique' in *Maison-Dieu*, xxiii, 1950, pp. 5–30, esp. 10; and in *Theol. Revue*, lii, 1956, pp. 6 f.
[6] J. Bidez, *Julian der Abtrünnige*, 4th ed., Munich, 1940, p. 284.

E

some understanding is indispensable for a living and spiritual religion.

There is, then, prayer in which words are of secondary
importance, in which the words serve to keep us in the
presence of God. Even today we frequently come upon the
case when the Breviary can do no more for the exhausted
pastor than keep him dimly in the presence of God for a
certain length of time. During that time, however, some
seed of the word of God may well fall upon fertile soil and
grow up to become a real encounter with God.[7]

But the fact remains that forms of thought and of language are given the task of supporting and nourishing
prayer.[8] It is still true that common prayer especially relies
upon the articulate word and upon noble forms, and can be
accounted for only thus; for in public worship we stand
before the majesty of God. Hence we have a duty to do all
in our power to provide public worship with the finest form
possible, and to create the best conditions we can for prayer.
At public worship we stand in communion with our brethren whom we must consider; and it is precisely by the
spoken word of prayer that we should support and help one
another.

Cardinal Suhard has made a very pertinent comment:
'When the religious life in any society is on the wane, it
flees into the liturgy; when it is on the increase it draws
its strength from the liturgy and moves outwards.'[9] That
is to say: the traditional forms of the liturgy form the natural
foundation for religious renewal.

At this point we may refer to one or two chief require-

[7] Admittedly, when all that remains is the intention to fulfil an obligation, the
result may be that through the Breviary the priest 'unlearns the art of prayer' – as
many have complained already. Cf. M. Pfliegler, *Priesterliche Existenz*, Innsbruck,
1958, p. 116.

[8] Cf. the remarks of St Thomas, *Summa Th.* IIa IIae, q. 83, a. 12, ad 1: prayer is
said aloud *quod mens orantis vel aliorum excitetur in Deum*.

[9] Cardinal Suhard, *Aufsteig oder Niedergang der Kirche?* Offenburg, 1947, p. 67.

ments which must be fulfilled if corporate public worship
is to unfold its renovating power. The first is the conviction
that the liturgy is not, as the older view of liturgy probably
assumed, simply a complex of rites and formularies which
must be correctly performed, so that a specific grace-giving
effect, in sacrament or sacramental, be produced. Liturgy
is, rather, a service of God in which men's hearts are raised
up to God. It is often supposed that being devout is an
activity additional to the liturgy itself; but we must affirm
the principle that we can and ought to express our devotion
in and through the liturgy,[10] and that the liturgy, in the well-
known words of Pius X, is actually the first and irreplace-
able source from which the faithful draw the Spirit of
Christ.[11] Liturgy in its entirety has grown out of religious
life. It is a storehouse of the religious life of centuries,
stored up in forms, it is true, that were appropriate to
these past ages, and which, in the course of development,
have often become overlaid with secondary structures that
are not always helpful. However that may be, in order that
these forms, which we do not want arbitrarily to set aside,
may speak to us, wherever possible they must be brought
into the open and performed with all the care and reverence
their content deserves. Moreover, they must be made available to all of the faithful.

The liturgical movement has tried a whole series of
possibilities along these lines: the extension of the use of
Missals, various forms of vernacular participation at Mass.
Other possibilities will occur as further research in these
matters is completed. In order that we may not achieve a
merely external participation in actions, words, and singing,
the right kind of preaching of the faith must be added. That

[10] This was the theme of the second German liturgical Congress in Munich in
1955. The reports were published in the *Liturgisches Jahrbuch*, v, 1955, pp. 69–194.
[11] *Motu proprio*, 22 November 1903, in *A.A.S.*, xxxvi, 1903–4, pp. 331, 338.

is why this is the main theme of this book. At the same time, in the forms of the celebration of public worship care must be taken to ensure the greatest possible clarity and simplicity, consonant with current prescriptions. It was no accident that at the start of the liturgical movement in German-speaking countries, the book used for the elementary instruction of beginners was Romano Guardini's *Sacred Signs*, which discussed the very simplest topics: standing, walking, the sign of the cross, holy water, and other similar non-spectacular matters. It is these primary elements that are best able to kindle true devotion.

It has been correctly affirmed that the opening up of access to ancient usages will not provide the men of today with a way into religious life.[12] This is especially true when these usages are complicated. Historical explanation of the liturgy cannot hope to make every detail of the traditional liturgy intelligible to the average Christian; its purpose is rather to lead us back to the basic conceptions that all can understand and which should be stressed as far as possible, until a far-reaching reorganization can bring them once again into their own. One of the happiest signs in the liturgical life of this century is this impulse towards simplicity, to what is essential, to what is practicable for the straightforward modern man, in the forms which should to some extent provide the sounding-board for the language of prayer. Church architecture has become liberated from the decorative forms inherited from past ages, and now attempts simply to provide a space appropriate for an assembled congregation whose attention is directed towards the altar. Once again the altar has become a table, and this fact is not obscured by any superstructure. Vestments reflect the fact that they are garments worn at Mass. Even quite simple symbols, which we were accustomed to see copiously applied to vestments, are now used with restraint. In the field of music, the great polyphonic art-song, in spite of its apparent excellence, is retreating to special feast-days and to centres of special culture: simple congregational singing is on the increase everywhere.

Finally, this simplicity and clarity is but the external sign of a deeper feature of all true public worship; reverence before the august and holy majesty of God. It is no accident that even in our inherited liturgy (and in almost every liturgy), and in the wider circle of the sanctuary too, where poetry and music are permitted to offer their riches in praise of God, language, when used in the direct encounter between man at prayer and the infinite God – i.e. in the prayer of the priest – never exceeds the limits of restrained prose. This is an expression of our sense for what is holy, and is a fundamental condition and the basic constitution of all genuine prayer. Admittedly this basic constitution is seriously threatened in man today, for he thinks that he has penetrated all the mysteries of nature and mastered all its powers, and that he can direct everything according to his own will. All the more, therefore, must common worship strive to deepen this sense of the holy, and to foster the spirit of adoration before him who has freely given us all that we have, who has made us what we are.

XIV

The People at Prayer

WHEN WE turn to examine the verbal expression of prayer it will surprise us not a little to find in the liturgical sphere, apart from the Eucharist, only the canonical office, which, in its modern form, is designed for the clergy and religious. Within the liturgy no real provision is made for the laity. It is indeed a marvellous thing to see – especially in the Middle Ages – how groups of men cut themselves off from the generality of mankind, and, without entering the special service of the Church, reduced their worldly requirements to the minimum so as to live more for eternal things. These were the monks. In addition there was the collegiate chapter of clergy, formed upon the monastic model. The Christian laity who had to go about their daily business regarded these as men taken from their midst, whose task was to offer prayer to God on their behalf, forging a permanent link between heaven and earth by their almost uninterrupted prayer. These men had to be magnanimously supported, therefore, by the faithful. The freedom from earthly care that resulted sometimes proved exceedingly dangerous for the religious. For the people, too, this notion of being represented at prayer had its dangers: it could lead to a complete abandonment of all responsibility.

The Hours of Prayer, the Office, grew out of the ancient Christian prayers at set hours. We have plenty of evidence that in the second, third, and fourth centuries Christians, even those at work in the world, sanctified the chief moments of the day and night by these prayers. Not only was prayer offered morning and evening, but there were moments of meditation at the third, sixth, and ninth hours, and at midnight, when the corresponding stages in our Lord's Passion and glorification were recommended as appropriate points of meditation for different hours. Especially after the Church ceased to be persecuted, the morning and evening Hours came to be celebrated in the larger churches, as a more developed form of corporate daily public worship, in which the clergy acted merely as leaders. For their part the monks extended the liturgical form to all of the Hours. In this way the canonical Hours arose as we find them in our Breviary. For centuries, down to modern times, this has regularly been celebrated in choir. It has been celebrated thus not only in monastic churches and cathedral chapters, but also in countless collegiate chapters in cities and in the country, and, with the assistance of scholars, in parish churches too (but only in important centres). At first it was obligatory only as a choral office; and only those who belonged to a church which had the choral office but could not be present at it, were obliged to recite it in private, using the Breviary which has been devised for that purpose.[1] In the form of choral prayer, performed with specialized functions, with singing and a fixed ceremonial, the canonical Office of clergy and monks became the subject of a high liturgical culture. Every antiphon, every modification of a verse which had to correspond to the course of the Christian Year, every movement and every bowing of the head, was exactly prescribed. But it was the very height of this culture – the basis of which naturally was Latin – which prevented the people from taking part, even if from long-standing custom they still came to Matins and Vespers. The only things they could understand were the fine melodies, the orderly movements, the rising incense.

---

[1] P. Salmon, 'Die Verpflichtung zum kirchlichen Stundengebet' in *Brevierstudien*, ed. J. A. Jungmann, Trier, 1958, pp. 85–116.

It is a striking fact that in the course of the centuries nothing was ever done to provide a substitute for the faithful according to their own capacities. The morality plays of the late Middle Ages, confined to special festivals and to large centres, were no such substitute; nor were the collections of prayers and the prayerbooks, which were mostly in Latin, available to very few people, and designed for private use by individuals.[2] There was obvious impoverishment here. Not until the Middle Ages were passed did an evening service suited to the people gradually emerge in various places out of afternoon devotions in addition to Vespers, with the *Salve Regina* and the sacramental blessing as its centre. Again this applied only to Sundays and feast-days. Beyond this, apart from Mass, there was no officially regulated prayer for the bulk of the faithful.[3] And so, for their prayer, the faithful were thrown back upon a few ancient, traditional basic formulae. The tradition must have come down from antiquity, that the Christian begin and end his day's work with the two basic prayers which had been given to him at baptism – the Our Father and the Creed.[4] In the Carolingian Renaissance it was insisted that every Christian should know these by heart.

In order to be able to fill up a set length of time with prayer, there was the possibility of repetition.[5] The Irish repeated the genuflexion – they had daily practices which included 100 or 300 genuflexions. This devotion spread on

---

[2] Cf. J. Leclercq, 'Dévotion privée, piété populaire et liturgique au moyen-âge' in *Études de pastoral liturgique* (*Lex orandi*, 1, Paris, 1944), pp. 149–83.

[3] In earlier times it was probably only the narrower circles of the brotherhoods that practised daily prayer, which was orientated in some degree upon the canonical Hours, and which made use of the psalms and hymns, as is seen in the Little Book of Hours of the declining Middle Ages. The Little Office of the Blessed Virgin is the best-known example of this sort of thing.

[4] J. A. Jungmann, *Gewordene Liturgie*, Innsbruck, 1941, pp. 165–72.

[5] For documentation see Jungmann, *Pastoral Liturgy*, pp. 172–80. A more exhaustive study of sources is given by W. Godel, O.S.B., 'Irisches Beten im frühen Mittelalter' in *Zeitschrift für katholische Theologie*, LXXXV, 1963.

the continent as well. The genuflexion was associated with the ejaculation: 'Lord, have mercy upon me' or 'Lord, forgive my sins' or even by the Our Father. We learn from Regino of Prüm (d. 915) of a penitent who had to perform seventy genuflexions and Our Fathers in one day. Forms developed, on the model of the 150 psalms, comprising 150 Our Fathers, or one third of that number. From the twelfth century these were replaced by the *Ave Maria* which was repeated in the same way. And so, with the addition of a *Pater noster* at each decade, out of this emerged the Marian Psalter – the Rosary.

In the Rosary, especially once it had become enriched by its well-known introduction and association with the mysteries of our redemption, we had reached a timeless form of prayer, classical in its own way; but there remained, in addition to the above-mentioned repetition of a formula or group of formulae, the customary device of giving prayer a certain time-span, when richer texts were lacking. In this the substitute character of such forms of prayer again becomes clear. According to the twelfth-century *Liber usuum* of the Cistercians, when one of the brethren died, every cleric in the community had to say the whole Psalter. Only those who could not do this were allowed to recite the *Miserere* 150 times, and if this was beyond their powers, the Our Father 150 times.[6] Similarly the Franciscan rule prescribes that the lay-brothers recite a number of Our Fathers in place of the canonical Hours, the number being appropriate to the Hour – for example, twenty-four in place of Matins.[7] Correspondingly, the third orders, too, knew the distinction between those who could say the Breviary

[6] *Liber usuum,* IV, 99 (*P. L.* CLXVI, 1478 ff.). A few more examples are noted in the *Zeitschrift für katholische Theologie,* LXXIII, 1951, p. 354.

[7] Further examples in Ph. Hofmeister, 'Chor- und Brevierpflichten bei den Ordensleuten mit feierlichem Gelübden' in *Liturgisches Jahrbuch,* x, 1960, pp. 10–28. Thus the lay-brothers' office in the Carthusian order contained eighty-three Our Fathers daily.

or an equivalent number of psalms, and those who could not read. These made do with the Our Father.[8] The same method of substitution was applied to more recent forms of devotion also.[9]

It is long-standing custom to repeat a single formula, a short ejaculation, a word of praise, within the liturgy itself. The Alleluia is one example. In the old Spanish liturgy of Good Friday the cry of *Indulgentiam* went up from the faithful up to 300 times. In the same way the *Kyrie eleison* was and is repeated in various liturgies, *ad lib.* or a set number of times – 12, 40, 100.[10] Such repetition expresses the depth and fervour of the substance of the ejaculation. Clearly a short petition is more suitable for repetition than a complex formula. To this category belongs the ejaculation, of which tradition provides a great store. All that is required is a proper selection and appropriate development.[11]

It is more difficult when what has to be repeated is a group of formulae not at all unified in itself. There may be a purely external link between two accidentally concurrent formulae, as when in the late Middle Ages it became almost

[8] Not until Leo XIII was it prescribed that the laity, in so far as they did not use the Breviary or the Little Office of our Lady, should say twelve Our Fathers, Aves, and Glorias, daily – F. Beringer, *Die Ablässe*, II, 15th ed., Paderborn, 1922, pp. 401 f.

[9] A devotional book of the eighteenth century provides a novena in honour of St Antony, adding: 'Whoever cannot read should recite the Our Father, the Hail Mary, and the Gloria, devoutly nine times.' J. Beczkowsky, *Die betrübte und nach ihrem Geliebten seufzende Turtel-Taube*, Nürnberg, 1704; also G. Schreiber, *Die Wochentage*, Cologne, 1959, pp. 133 f.

[10] An account from the time of Otto III (d. 1002) tells of a procession when *Kyrie eleison, Christe eleison*, and finally *Kyrie eleison* were said a hundred times each before a picture of Christ. M. Andrieu, *Les Ordines Romani*, v, Louvain, 1961, p. 358. There are other examples in Jungmann, 'Flectere pro Carolo rege' in *Mélanges Andrieu*, Strassburg, 1956, p. 221.

[11] An apposite example is provided by a prayer-card published by the St Benno-Verlag in Leipzig (1955): 'The Everlasting Prayer to Christ.' This takes the responsory from Prime, 'Christ, thou Son of the living God, have mercy on us!' as its foundation, and in a following verse, as in the Breviary, varies this for every Sunday and feast-day in the year, as a rule making use of some title-phrase from the appropriate Gospel.

the rule[12] to append the *Ave Maria* to the Our Father as though it were an *Embolismus* like the *Libera nos, quaesumus, Domine* of the Mass – although, with Canisius,[13] we can provide an acceptable reason for this. The multiple repetition of the double form thus evolved is not easy to accomplish with devotion. No one can possibly repeat the Our Father, *Ave,* and *Gloria* six times over, in such a way as to allow the mind to follow the words step by step, or even to recite them with devotion as is prescribed for the *Toties-quoties* indulgence.[14]

What has been said is meant only to point out that things could be a lot better with regard to what is provided for our people in the way of prayer apart from the Eucharist. In the private prayers of the faithful the same one or two formulae are being constantly repeated. The Lord's Prayer forms the permanent basis, that is still constantly being illumined and expounded by edifying literature. Since the late Middle Ages the *Ave Maria* has become common property everywhere. For a time the *Confiteor,* or its free translation in the vernacular – general confession of sin – was another favourite.[15] Catechisms added many more, and the universal catechizing of children provides opportunity of inculcating in children the things that are important. In addition, the vernacular part of parish Mass – the prayers after the sermon,

[12] See *Zeitschrift für katholische Theologie,* LXXIII, 1951, pp. 355–7.

[13] *Ibid.,* pp. 356 f.

[14] The requirement of this prayer in order to gain the *Toties-quoties* indulgence of the Portiuncula (and on other occasions also) has been in effect only since 1924: *A.A.S.,* XVI, 1924, p. 347; cf. *ibid.* XXII, 1930, p. 363; XXIV 1932, pp. 231 ff. Until that date there had been freedom in the choice of prayers. This regulation is understandable only as a return to a form of prayer hallowed by early Franciscan usage. In the third order there was an occasional mitigation of even the above-mentioned Our Father. Instead of its having to be said thrice in succession, each petition might be repeated thrice. Out of this practice a hymn was produced – A. Gundlach, *Verklärung des Herrn,* Munich, 1957, p. 70.

[15] The French reforming synods of 1629–30 required all the faithful to know the *Pater noster, Ave, Credo,* and *Confiteor* – P. Broutin, *La reforme pastoral en France au XVIIe siécle,* Paris, 1950, I, p. 151.

for example – contain much that the faithful might well take over into their own treasury of prayer.[16]

One of the most pressing pastoral problems in this field will be to satisfy the needs of family prayer, or the practice of daily prayer, which is partly coextensive with it. It has always been taken for granted that the Christian should begin and end the day with prayer. These prayers ought not to become complicated, but should be principally an adoring glance towards God, and a humble, grateful, backward glance to God, expressed in a simple and straightforward manner.[17] In grace at meals we acknowledge our creatureliness and our dependence in a thousand ways upon the gifts of God's providence. One of the alarming signs of the secularization of life is that even Christian families neglect to say grace at meals.

Ought we to lay much store by the thrice daily prayer which the Angelus bell still announces in Christian countries? It would be a great pity if this never happened at all, and if the Angelus became an empty form. Prayer when the Angelus is sounded is a late offshoot from that tradition according to which the faithful in the ancient Church were required to say the Our Father thrice a day (*Didache*, c. 8, 3), and according to which in later centuries they commemorated the stations of our Lord's passion at the appropriate three hours of the day, and his resurrection during the night. We can trace this tradition right through the Middle

---

[16] Amongst these are the acts of Faith, Hope, and Charity. The form of these prayers, however, betrays the fact that they are rigidly derived from theological definitions. Criticisms of this are to be found in Jungmann, *Die Frohbotschaft und unsere Glaubensverkündigung*, Regensburg, 1936, pp. 105 ff. Since the present book was written, the prayers after the sermon at Mass have been changed in form. Now we have, after the Creed, the Prayer of the Faithful, modelled on the ancient litanies.

[17] It is instructive that a questionnaire addressed to Catholic men in Cologne revealed that out of 189, ninety-seven still used Luise Hensel's evening hymn 'Müde bin ich, geh' zur Ruh' as their evening prayer – a prayer they must have learned in childhood – H. Ostermann, 'Über das Gebetsleben des kirchentreuen Mannes' in *Geist und Leben*, XXXII, 1959, pp. 292–301.

Ages, the only difference being that the Resurrection came in the end to be commemorated at the morning hour, and in the evening the topic came to be the Annunciation.[18] Midday was retained as the time for the commemoration of the Crucifixion.[19] As late as 1605 we find the Synod of Prague stressing this threefold apportioning of topics: but the topics are now viewed in a Marian light and are linked at each hour with the *Angelus Domini* as we know it today.[20] Thus the mystery of the Incarnation had taken the place of the earlier commemoration of the Passion, just as Christmas had overshadowed Easter in the popular imagination.

At the same time, however, a popular commemoration of the Passion had evolved in the course of the week.[21] On Thursday evening after the Angelus came the commemoration of our Lord's death-agony; on Friday 'at the Ninth Hour' came the commemoration of his death upon the cross (earlier it has been 'at the Sixth Hour' in many places – the hour of the Crucifixion), associated in many places with the tolling of the great bell as a call to prayer, for which there are many traditional texts.[22] Although a straightforward return to the threefold commemoration of the Passion may not be necessary, at least we might hear the toll of the bell calling us to prayer on Thursday and Friday evening.

In 1947 the Union of German Catholic Youth declared the Angelus to be its prayer: the Angelus was to be said

[18] Cf. J. Stadlhuber, 'Das Laienstundengebet vom Leiden Christi in seinem mittelalterlichen Fortleben' in *Zeitschrift für katholische Theologie*, LXXII, 1950, pp. 282–325.

[19] *Ibid.*, p. 309.

[20] Hartzheim, *Concilia Germaniae*, VIII, 1769, p. 741.

[21] Cf. above, p. 113.

[22] These have been preserved in the diocesan prayerbooks of southern Germany and Austria, and elsewhere, in the same texts, derived from the liturgy, as they had in the sixteenth century, and for the same occasions. Cf. information about Mount of Olives devotion and *Tenebrae* in G. Schreiber, *Die Wochentage*, Cologne, 1959, pp. 161 f., p. 172. On *Tenebrae* of Friday cf. also J. Greving, *Johann Ecks Pfarrbuch*, Münster, 1908, p. 123.

once a day.[23] To demand that it be recited thrice a day, at
every sounding of the Angelus-bell, would perhaps be too
big a demand to lay upon the average Christian, especially
if morning and evening prayer were already part of his
daily rule of life. Its performance in the hubbub of a busy
city street would be impossible. But it might well be possible, at home or even in the street, to carry out something
like the minute of recollection on Good Friday, as is
courageously done by the Young Catholic Workers in many
industries. When the bell tolls one keeps silent for a few
moments. Here the differentiation of commemoration
might be revived, in the medieval style: the thought of the
angel's message has always been kept principally for the
evening hour: rising in the morning would remain associated with Christ's resurrection, and the midday with his
passion.[24]

As well as private and family prayer at home, we must not
neglect the regular common prayer of the faithful in church,
other than the celebration of the Eucharist. Today this has
become threatened with almost complete collapse. Whereas
in early Christian times the faithful had a daily liturgy of
the Word, morning and evening, assembling only on
Sundays and feast-days to celebrate the climax and crown of
their life in the Eucharist, today we have reached the
opposite pole. We have the celebration of Mass every day:
only on Sundays and feast-days do we have devotions.
And now these devotions are being ousted by evening

[23] The diocesan Synod of Aachen wanted to ask the same of all Catholic families.
It added: 'Lessons of instruction, lectures, or other similar arrangements should be
interrupted when the Angelus calls to prayer.' *Dokumente zu den Diözesanstatuten des
Bistum Aachen* (Erste Diözesansynode Aachen, II), Aachen, 1960, p. 1120. The latter
prescription admittedly could not be carried out without qualification.

[24] It might be considered more correct and more promising to recommend a
change round to the chronological order which was still alive in people's minds at
the end of the sixteenth century as the threefold commemoration, and which
Cardinal Bellarmine recommends in his catechism: morning, the Annunciation;
midday, the Crucifixion; evening, the Resurrection.

Mass.[25] In many parishes even on Sunday, evening devotions appear as a precarious appendage to the evening Mass.

We do not say that the evening Mass is not necessary today in certain circumstances. We do ask, however, whether the superfluity of Masses at almost every hour of the day on Sundays and feast-days does not represent an inflation and hence a devaluation of the Mass, not least because in this way every helpful preparation falls into disuse. It is true that the Mass itself contains a preparation in its first section – in the liturgy of the Word; but this liturgy of the Word, unless it contains a homily and intercessions, is over in a few minutes and is compressed into too small a space, and so must be seen as a very inadequate solution. The healthy life of a parish demands more extended and free development along this line, even if only a fragment of the congregation attend.[26]

There is no lack of traditional forms of such evening devotions. There are devotions that have had their fixed form from time immemorial. In southern Germany and in Austria very often the Rosary with the addition of one of the litanies, or the Way of the Cross, is the traditional form in which afternoon or evening devotions have been provided.[27]

---

[25] The Roman *Instructio* (3 September 1958, n. 45) draws attention to this danger.

[26] *Constitution on the Sacred Liturgy* (Whitegate Publications, 1963), Chap. I, sec. III, C (4).

[27] As we know, many attempts are now being made to refurbish these tested forms of prayer. R. Guardini provides valuable stimulus towards the expansion of the Rosary: see especially *The Rosary of Our Lady*. Many things have already been taken up by diocesan prayerbooks and developed further in them. Cf. especially E. J. Lengeling's manual, *Gottesdienst*, supplied for the diocesan prayerbook of Münster (Münster, 1955), pp. 805–64. This adds a fourth to the normal three sets of mysteries of the rosary. They are called the 'mysteries of comfort': (1) Our Lord rules from heaven; (2) He lives and reigns in his Church; (3) He will judge the living and the dead; (4) He will make all things new and perfect all things; (5) He will be our eternal reward. This proposal is taken up by the diocesan prayerbook of Innsbruck also: *Gotteslob*, 1945, p. 419 f. H. Schürmann gives good advice. After each decade we should add the supplication, 'Pray for us, Queen of the holy Rosary!' and the collect for the feast of the holy Rosary (mentioning the appropriate mystery). Cf. the manual, *Quadragese und Pentekoste*, Trier, 1960, pp. 114 ff.

In other places there are popular devotions with a richly variable content, their main section being composed of meditation: Scripture-reading and prayer with edifying exposition of a doctrine or a topic. The founder of this type is said to have been Peter Canisius with his *Catechism and Prayerbook*. In other places again, the Rhineland especially, there is an older tradition in a devotion modelled on the Hours of the Office, and which somehow carries on the late medieval tradition of the Little Book of Hours. There is a hymn at the start, a collect introduced by a versicle at the end, no psalms, but the initial scheme repeated several times, with a mystery of the faith or the veneration of a saint as the central point.[28] Sundays and feast-days and their vigils are the best times for such devotions. Triduums, Forty Hours' Prayer, Novenas, and May devotions are other suitable occasions. When such devotions are carried out in church, and led by the pastor of the parish, all the requirements are fulfilled for the observance of the public worship of the Church, according to the traditional concept – if we exclude the prescriptions about form.[29]

At the same time we cannot deny that these devotions, in so far as they have not been revised in the diocesan prayerbooks of the last decades, have suffered much neglect and degeneration in form. Very often they show no connexion

[28] Th. Schnitzler, 'Stundengebet und Volksandacht' in *Brevierstudien*, Trier, 1958, pp. 71–84; *id.*, *Messopferfeier und Nachmittagsandacht*, 2nd ed., Freiburg, 1953, pp. 354–63.

[29] According to the fixed terminology of the *Instructio* of 3 September 1958, Church legislation henceforth regards as liturgy only what is done *secundum libros a Sancta Sede approbatos*. Devotions do not belong to this narrower group. In the devotions are not included worship prescribed by Rome for the universal Church – worship having papal legality – but worship having episcopal authority, called, in the said terminology, *pia exercitia*, does fall within the category of devotions. But their religious and theological value is by no means called in question. Cf. the evaluation of these devotions by the Second Vatican Council, *Constitution on the Sacred Liturgy* 1963, Chap. I, 1, 13. Their status in the Church's life is exactly the same as that of Matins and Vespers before the reform of Pius V (1568–70). Cf. Jungmann, 'Liturgie und *pia exercitia*' in *Liturgisches Jahrbuch*, IX, 1959, pp. 79–86.

with the Christian Year, or they have produced a Christian Year of their own.

Devotions formed in the style of meditations produce forms of prayer which often contradict the genuine nature of prayer. They are simply 'prayed catechism, instruction disguised in the garment of prayer.'[30] It is dishonest and undignified in this way to weave admonition, addressed to the congregation, into prayers addressed to God.

The devotions which show the influence of the Hours of the Office have all too often taken over merely the skeleton, the sequence of versicles and antiphons, instead of grasping the original structural law and so achieving perfect clarity. Prayers that may be good for the individual are not on that account appropriate for corporate devotion. Even if devotions cannot always maintain the cool austerity of the Roman collects, they must bear the character of objectivity; they must speak of things that apply to all in the same way, and dare not run away into floods of sentiment. For this reason the best prayers of the mystics are often unsuitable, even for private use.

It is not superfluous, therefore, to consider briefly the essential laws that apply here. These are found to be fundamentally the same as have governed corporate prayer in the Church from the very start. In content especially, these prayers must fulfil certain requirements. They must reflect the world of faith as it is. Hence they may not isolate a particular object in such a way that sight of the total reality is obscured. It is sound liturgical practice always to keep the whole picture there in the background, whatever the special topic of liturgical celebration – saint's feast-day or some other occasion. For the same reason, isolated incidents from salvation-history ought not to be projected into the present so as to disavow the real present, and the present reality of

[30] Th. Schnitzler, *Messopferfeier und Nachmittagsandacht*, p. 361.

the order of salvation. In Advent, our eyes fixed upon the coming kingdom, we can make our own the longing of our forefathers; but we are not back again in the Old Testament. We may adore the Christ-child in the crib, we may portray the obeisance of the shepherds before the divine child, and we may sing hymns in his praise;[31] but we cannot really pray to the Christ-child because Jesus is no longer a child; he is the *Kyrios* seated at the right hand of the Father. Similarly, as long as there are Christians upon this earth, Christian meditation will lose itself, with adoring reverence and compassion, in the Passion of our Lord; but on the other hand we must never forget that the sufferings and death are past: 'Christ has risen from the dead and dies no more; death has no longer dominion over him' (Rom. 6. 9). The piety of the late Middle Ages, about the year 1000, had immersed itself with growing fervour in the 'bitter Passion' of the Redeemer, had analysed the separate phases of this Passion, counted his wounds, and, in its art, portrayed with fearful realism the Man of Sorrows and the Crucified, but lost sight of the radiance of transfiguration and glory in which the Romanesque period had still known how to clothe him. The Middle Ages had walked along the Way of the Cross, but come to a halt at the laying in the tomb. Its darling theme was the *Christus patiens*. The preceding epoch too had known well the cross of the Lord, but its theme had been *Christus passus et gloriosus*.[32] Without doubt we must recognize the greater authenticity and reality of this older style of devotion. It does not run the risk of being satisfied with a partial aspect, of mistaking salvation-history for a purely past affair, thus falling into an 'as if'

---

[31] Even in hymns we ought not to introduce the intercession of our Lady as is done in the well-known hymn 'O Queen of Glory': 'Ask the babe in your arms to have mercy on us.'

[32] Cf. this contrast in J. Stadlhuber, *Das Laienstundengebet vom Leiden Christi in seinem mittelalterlichen Fortleben*, pp. 294, 305, 308, 314 ff.

state of mind when it tries to re-present the past. And so, efforts that are made to supplement Passion-piety along the lines of the older tradition, deserve every encouragement – as, for example, in the move to have a fifteenth station of the Resurrection added after the present fourteen stations of the cross.[33]

Common prayer must never be confused with sermons or catechisms, for it is addressed to God, not to men; but it should be so composed that in it the invisible world of faith shines, so that we are able, in the light of our knowledge of the faith, to approach God in confidence and love. In prayer, therefore, there must be a true expression of the image of God and of the relation in which man stands to him, as far as that image is accessible to us. In order that the image of God may assume its proper place, it is above all necessary that prayer, at least in its highest flights, should reach the goal of all prayer and not stop short at subordinate powers. Prayer is defined as the raising up of the mind and heart to God; but countless devotional practices as they have come down to us from recent generations, or as they are set out in prayerbooks, move entirely within the circle of their own particular devotion – a saint, the image of Mary, the Sacred Heart, the Holy Spirit. All too rarely does the high vault of heaven rise above the multiplicity of separate images and figures, supplying an all-embracing and all-supporting firmament. Such a wealth of forms of this greater prayer lies ready to hand. To begin with, there is the Our Father, if only we are allowed to feel its full intrinsic weight – as we are not when it is used simply as padding or as a coin, the value of which lies in the number of the pieces.

The Old Testament provides us with the psalms. These

---

[33] Cf. J. Gaillard in *Revue Thomiste*, LVI, 1956, p. 169; J. Hofinger, J. Kellner, *Liturgische Erneuerung in der Weltmission*, Innsbruck, 1957, p. 237.

are certainly not all suitable for use as corporate prayer, but
a selection of them are. That the psalms can become very
popular today is proved by the psalm-singing movement
that has gathered great momentum in France within a few
years, and has now spread to other countries as well. The
Little Breviaries which, in the space of a few years, have
been produced in several countries,[34] have provided a useful
selection ready for wider circles of worshippers. When
whole psalms are unsuitable, selected verses can be used.
The early Middle Ages had composed whole collections of
such *capitella de psalmis,* and obviously provided them for
the laity's use.[35]

One of the happy advances made in our time is that quite
a number of hymns, which have been composed on the
pattern of the psalms, or as paraphrases of the psalms, have
been included in diocesan hymn-books for use by the people,
so that now a hymn like the *Gloria in excelsis* can be known
by heart by every child, thanks to the community-Mass.
Finally, quite a number of the collects from the Missal can
be used in popular devotions, either verbatim, or as a pattern
for prayer.

At all events, in prayer the image of God should be expressed. In this the form of address which places us in the
presence of God is not without importance. In the Roman
liturgy as a rule only a few predicates are attached to the
name of God: *Omnipotens Deus, Omnipotens aeterne Deus.*
He bears all in his hands (omnipotens = παντοκράτωρ);
he is supreme above all the changes of time. On special
occasions a relative predication is added: *Deus qui hodierna
die* . . . , and this transports us immediately into a particular

---

[34] See the survey by H. Schmidt, *Introductio in liturgiam occidentalem*, Rome, 1960,
pp. 472–81. Concerning Germany in particular cf. P. Hildebrand Fleischmann,
Officium divinum parvum, 8th ed., 1958.

[35] One example is the Irish *Book of Cerne,* edited by Kuypers, Cambridge, 1902,
pp. 174–98.

aspect of the order of salvation. The Eastern liturgies use a richer language.

In the introductions to his argument St Paul likes to speak of 'God the Father of our Lord Jesus Christ.' To call first upon God and then upon Christ is a mark of our oldest hymns – the *Gloria in excelsis* and the *Te Deum*. The prayer-formulae of our devotion tend, where prayer is directed to God and to Christ, to add prayers, in like manner and in equal measure, to the Holy Spirit. This means, however, that in Christ we are seeing only the Son of God apart from his humanity. On the other hand, we complain, in the same sense no doubt, that the Holy Spirit is still 'the unknown God,' and in this way try to justify the complaint. We are going a step further when we isolate prayer to the Holy Spirit and address formal prayers to him. Zeal to express faith in the divine Persons by such forms of prayer arises from the anti-Arian feeling which influenced and twisted theological thinking and, in certain areas, the liturgical prayer of the early Middle Ages.[36] The ancient Church had acted differently. It recalled our relationship to God according to the economy of redemption: we love the Father through the Son in the Holy Spirit. Where these ancient heresies have lost their virulence, this feeling ought now to give way to a more balanced attitude. Today we do find this sort of adjustment in progress.[37] It is true that there are liturgies in which the collects address the Trinity, or the concluding doxology names the three divine Persons; but collects which address the Holy Spirit have never been normal. Even the *Epiclesis* of the Eastern liturgy has never

[36] Cf. above, p. 34 f.

[37] In this century we have witnessed an example of this kind of adjustment in the sphere of the Creed. The Athanasian Creed, *Quicumque*, which used to be said daily in many Carolingian churches (e.g. the abbey of Theodulf of Orleans, d. 821), and which, until the time of Pius X had to be recited every Sunday at Prime, was confined by Pius X to Sundays without a double commemoration, and by the rubrical reform of 1955 has now been confined to Trinity Sunday.

been a prayer *to* the Holy Spirit, but always a prayer *for*
the Holy Spirit.[38] Only in the freer language of poetry, in
hymns and antiphons, is the Holy Spirit called down, is he
asked to come, because in him we recognize the uncreated
grace for which we long. The three Persons are one God,
one majesty, and one object of adoration, the one giver
of all good things. Therefore, according to the older laws
of form, we ought, in order to avoid giving the impression
of tritheism, never to call upon one divine Person without
calling upon the others. Even when prayer mentions God
the Father, the ultimate origin, the Son and the Holy Spirit
are included: we are speaking of the one God.[39] At a later
phase of development when it had become customary to
invoke each of the divine Persons separately at the beginning
of the litanies,[40] this was by no means taken for granted;
it had to be justified by the explanation that in these God
was being invoked under the names of the three Persons.[41]

If the world of faith is to be reflected in the language of
common prayer, this applies specially to the relationship in
which we stand to God. We are not strangers to God, still
less seekers who do not know whether their cry will be heard.
In Christ, God has come to us. In his Church he has set up
his kindgom upon earth. In his Son's words we are permitted to say 'Our Father!' This awareness must be alive in
the faithful when they enter church to engage in common
prayer. It affects even the shape of the church-building.
When the faithful of Christian antiquity entered the
basilica, their eyes were drawn forward by the row of

---

[38] A few isolated exceptions in marginal areas are noted by Jungmann, *Die
Stellung Christi im liturgischen Gebet*, 2nd ed., Münster, 1962, p. 251 (Index).

[39] Cf. Karl Rahner, *Theological Investigations*, 1, pp. 125–30.

[40] The origin of this practice, which did not spread upon the continent until the
end of the tenth century, lay in the practice of the ancient Irish monks. W. Godel,
O.S.B. 'Irisches Beten im frühen Mittelalter' in *Zeitschrift für katholische Theologie*,
LXXXV, 1963, Books II and III.

[41] Details in Jungmann, *The Mass of the Roman Rite*, p. 228.

pillars; from the apse above the altar they were greeted by the picture of the new creation – Christ the Lord, the Shepherd, the King, and shining behind him, the new Jerusalem. Contemporary Church art, which has already achieved so much in the field of church architecture, has not yet reached the peak of its achievement in the formation of the style of building required. All the more must the Christian relationship to God come into play in the formulation of common prayer. In his letter to the Ephesians St Paul concludes his hymn in praise of the work of redemption and of the mercy of God with: 'To him be glory in the church and in Christ Jesus' (Eph. 3. 21).

This sounds that accord which should govern the Church's prayer from beginning to end. Christian antiquity incorporated the reference to the mediatorial office of Christ as a fixed element into the prayer of the Church. In this way it created the classic form of prayer, which the Roman liturgy has so faithfully preserved. We have access to God through Jesus Christ: *per Christum Dominum nostrum*. Those people to whom it was self-evident that prayer ought to contain such a reference must have kept the transformation of the world, which had come about through Christ, and through Christ alone, very much in the forefront of their minds. Even in circles acquainted with the liturgical revival, such a thing has as yet reached nothing like the intensity of these early times. To be a Christian means to have found a link with Christ and to be able, therefore, to look up to God, free from all anxiety and with complete trust. This same awareness is also the explanation of the above-mentioned style of following the praise of God in hymns with the invocation of Christ: *Tu rex gloriae Christi; Benedictus qui venit in nomine Domini*. In addition, this explains – although not quite so plainly – the rule which makes a litany to Christ, it may be, precede the prayers of the priest – as we find in a truncated form in the Roman liturgy, when the Our Father is introduced by the *Kyrie eleison, Christe eleison, Kyrie eleison.* The freshness and aliveness of that awareness is shown by the variety of its expressions. Even the *per Christum* does not appear as an invariable concluding formula in ancient Christian sources. It appears at the beginning or in the middle of a prayer as well as at the end; and it takes various forms: *per summum sacerdotem nostrum J. Chr.; per sacerdotem aeternum J. Chr.; per Dominum nostrum.*

Reference to Christ the Mediator is not the only way of expressing the new relationship to God that he has created. Reference to the Church can be used in the same way. The Church is the community of those who are called by God in Christ, whom God has made his people. To be a living member of the Church is to stand in the grace of God, to be his child. Hence in the prayer-texts of Hippolytus of Rome, besides the mediatorial form 'through thy servant Jesus Christ,' we find another: 'in thy Church.' Eastern liturgies show several variations of this thought. The Canon of the East Syrian Mass sounds this note: 'We would thank thee and praise thee eternally within thy Church which is redeemed in the blood of thy anointed . . . now and for ever and in all eternity.'[42] In the Armenian liturgy the deacon begins one prayer by inviting the congregation 'to entreat our Lord through the holy Church . . . ' and the priest, after the people's response, takes up the prayer in the words: 'In the midst of thy temple and in the presence of these divine and radiant signs and in this holy place . . .'[43]

There can be no doubt that believing awareness of nearness to God in Christ is expressed in less explicit forms. Marian devotion, too, and veneration of the saints, presuppose the knowledge that we do not face the divine majesty

---

[42] F. Brightman, *Liturgies Eastern and Western*, Oxford, 1896, p. 288.
[43] *Ibid.*, p. 416.

without a mediator; but this is a secondary expression. Quite apart from the tendency to isolate – a tendency that often appears – the predominant awareness of God and the Madonna, as we find in certain areas, is not at all in harmony with the reality of the Christian order. In its practical piety, the later Middle Ages had already transferred the concept of mediation to the saints in far too unbalanced a manner, and this led to that uneasy restlessness which was for ever seeking new patrons, new supports, and fresh assurances.

It may well be that where there is simple faith and devotion, the form of prayers matters little; but in the situation we are in now we must lay great stress upon what is eternally valid, and upon the greatest possible clarity of order. We need not exclude all secondary mediators, nor do these have to be subordinated to the primary Mediator in a strictly arranged hierarchy, indeed they should not be. It is only a supposititious theology that tries to introduce the saints as intercessors with our Lady, and our Lady as intercessor with her divine Son. We do better if we keep to the language of our liturgy, which sees our Lady and the saints as one mighty choir at prayer, who by their company intensify the divinely appointed mediation of Christ: *intercedente beata et gloriosa Virgine Maria cum omnibus Sancis tuis per Christum Dominum nostrum.*

In the style and formularies of our prayers we should aim at achieving the most practical arrangement possible. This is a very different thing both from rationalistic sobriety and theological complexity. How salutary it is for him who recites the Breviary to lose himself, on a feast of our Lady, in the *Officium Beatae Virginis*. Whatever he reads in the psalms remains the praise of God; but in this Office he finds psalms which tell of God's condescension to man and his care of the holy city, and which praise him for his mighty deeds, which tell exultantly also how man is able to reach up to the most holy God. All of this is summed up in a single amazement at God's choice of the Blessed Virgin, an amazement which is constantly finding expression in hymns and responsories, but which never breaks up the context as an isolated fact. In the lessons the mystery of the feast is doctrinally more precisely defined, and everything flows in the end into the collect in which we entreat God's help and grace through the intercession of the glorious and Blessed Virgin; but in the end all is asked in accordance with the fixed order of redemption – through Jesus Christ our Lord.

In popular piety there is no lack of examples which display a marvellous wealth of basic ideas, quite simply expressed. There is, to name but one, the translation of the *Regina Coeli:*

> Queen of Heaven, be joyful; alleluia!
> The son thou wast found worthy to bear – alleluia!
> Has risen from the dead, as he foretold; alleluia!
> Pray for us to God; alleluia!

The same kind of experience comes with the Litany of the Saints, where the horizon could scarcely be wider. In prayer we invoke a whole host of people from every rank in the Church triumphant; we mention, as titles to our hope, every phase in our Lord's life and death; every concern of the Church and of the individual earthly pilgrim throughout the whole of this world and the next is brought into the prayer. Psalms and antiphonal prayers are there too, and these intensify the corporate nature of the supplication. Here, too, the growing stream of this multitude of invocations flows out into the mighty ocean of the great prayer of the Church, which on this occasion seems to require a number of collects in order to be satisfied.

XV

Laws of Structure

IN ALL that has been said so far, we have merely stressed a
few points which deserve attention when we set about
forming non-eucharistic public worship, especially with
regard to its content. Even when these points are taken into
account, unless there is some other principle at work also,
a process can still go on, by which all the various elements
at our disposal – lessons, hymns, psalms, silent prayer,
litanies, collects – are simply lined up, so that the greatest
possible variety is the only result. For the time being it may
be that this method avoids exhausting the congregation
and arouses in them a host of ideas; the multiplicity may,
however, do nothing but create confusion. The faithful
should go home happy and edified, taking with them
not only a true, but also a clear, picture of the world of
faith. To achieve this the structure of any devotion, any
celebration, any evening service, must correspond to the
structural laws which flow from the nature of such an
activity of the Church. These structural laws can be fixed
only in the broadest outlines, so that plenty of scope is left
for individual variation, for the occasion of the assembly
and the peculiarities of those assembled must be taken into
account. The main lines are set, however, by the fact that the
Church, the people of God, are gathered together for the
public worship of God.

For a start something ought to happen so that the people
of God may be not just actually assembled, but become
aware of having been brought together by God. To some
extent this is achieved by the mere fact of being together

in the house of God. It is fully achieved if God stands at the beginning of the celebration as the one who invites. From the beginning of time it is he who has called the Church together. Grace and redemption proceed from him, not from men. It is fitting, therefore, for the word of God, the lesson, to stand at the beginning of the assembly. The word of God might be explained and interpreted at that point. At all events it should be able to find a reverberation in the hearts of the congregation, whether through the immediate response of an appropriate chant, as we find in our Roman liturgy, in which the lesson is regularly followed by a responsory, or by allowing a period of silence to follow, during which the word of God can sink more deeply into all hearts. But this is supposed to be an assembling for prayer too. Having heard God's word, the congregation must be allowed to raise their voice in prayer, and to present their desires and needs before God. This must be done, however, as a congregation, for the people have gathered together as a congregation, a tiny section of the people of God, reproducing in itself the structure of the whole Church: a people set under divinely appointed leadership. And so what is expressed should be the prayer of an assembled company, whether that be done by an alternation of spoken words or in periods of silence. In every case, however, the prayers of many should finally be summed up by the priestly leader of the assembly and thus presented to God. In fact such a plan lies, more or less clearly visible and more or less fully developed, beneath all the prayer of the Church, at least in so far as the congregation is an assembly of the faithful and not simply a monastic community. This ground-plan can be seen with special distinctness at many points in the Roman liturgy.[1]

[1] Cf. J. A. Jungmann, *Die liturgische Feier*, 3rd ed., Regensburg, 1961, pp. 59 ff. This book only sketches the topic, but a more detailed study chiefly with respect

In the separate canonical Hours the chief section begins –
if we set aside the psalmody of the first section – with the
Capitulum. This represents an abbreviated lesson. Then
comes a chant, usually in the form of a responsory, in many
cases (Lauds, Vespers) in the form of a hymn. Then the
transition to prayer is accomplished. Today, in rare cases
and usually reduced to a vestige, it must be admitted, this
prayer unfolds in the *Preces,* the responsorial prayer of the
community. This is concluded with the collect, in all cases
said by the officiant. This same plan can still be recognized
in rudimentary form in the liturgy of the Word at Mass.
The first lesson is followed by the responsorial Gradual,
and after the Gospel lesson comes the call to prayer, the
former *oratio communis*. On occasions when a celebration
went on for a long time, as in the vigils of the early Church,
we find this plan repeated several times. In the present
Foremass of Ember Saturdays it is repeated six times, in the
liturgy of Holy Saturday as still found in our Missal it is
repeated four times, on condition that the prayer of the
people is not provided for in the form of *Preces,* but as
silent prayer offered kneeling, which, according to ancient
Roman tradition is announced with *Flectamus genua* and
ended with *Levate*.

One further comment must be made about the elements
in this structure.

In our devotions the word of God is treated rather like a
step-mother. Compared with the conditions of the period
when the corporate observance of the morning and evening
Hour was flourishing, and with the importance which the

to the Eastern liturgies will be found in 'Die Rolle der Lesungen im Gemeinde-
offizium orientalischer Riten' (1962) in *Trierer theologischen Studien* by Jungmann's
pupil, R. Zerfass. This book provides an important elucidation of the historical
derivation attempted by Jungmann, by demonstrating that the ground-plan was
indeed applicable to the congregational office, but *not* to the monastic office, in so
far as the lesson was concerned.

lesson, the Scripture lesson in particular, enjoyed in those days, this state of affairs is in some measure understandable. In those days when every book was a manuscript and hence very costly, most people had no opportunity of hearing the word of God except at corporate public readings. Today printed books are to be found plentifully in every home. Even if only a small fraction of Catholic families make a habit of reading the Scriptures or the New Testament, it is through the great stream of Church newspapers and other religious literature that the written word of Scripture or its exposition and application reaches the great mass of the faithful. At the same time the demand is justified and obvious, that the word of God should have its rightful place when the Church meets together, above all in the liturgy of the Word of the Sunday Mass. But it should also have its place, as the normal practice, in every other fully developed service of public worship. An evening sermon is certainly an un-exceptionable form of presenting the word of God. Where, as is so often the case, this is out of the question, there should be the *Capitulum* from Holy Scripture or, as occasion demands, a spiritual reading from some other source.

In like manner the word of God could be made to enrich many other functions for which the Ritual makes provision. Consider, for example, the blessing of a new house – a most important family occasion. For this the Roman Ritual provides a single prayer (VIII, 6 and 7), or, as a solemn form, the *Miserere* with a prayer (VIII, 5). The bareness of the rite is specially felt when the occasion is the opening of a public institution or building project, the blessing of a bridge, or the laying of a foundation-stone. For all such occasions the official formula displays the same bareness. But the celebration takes on a totally different colour, it becomes more clearly incorporated in the great context of salvation-history, if an appropriate reading from Holy

Scripture precedes the prayers, thus bringing the whole ceremony more closely in line with the ground-plan of the liturgy.

In recent years in France there has been lively discussion as to whether it is right to bring straight back to the Mass, with its deep mysteries, men from a dechristianized background, who are beginning to turn back to the Church, or children from an environment in which they have never heard of God, but who are now coming to catechism. Might it not be more suited to their spiritual make-up, and in line with organic education, to prepare them by some sort of Mass of Catechumens?[2] The French bishops decided that preparatory arrangements should indeed be encouraged, but at the same time called attention to the obligation upon all to hear Sunday Mass, an obligation which also includes a right possessed by every baptized person.[3] The mysterious sacrifice of the New Covenant does not have to be grasped in all its depth, especially not by children; here too there are steps gradually leading up to fuller and fuller participation. It still remains true, however, that an independent, freely adapted liturgy of the Word could provide a most valuable preparation.

Conversely, the word of God, the word of Holy Scripture in particular, where it is presented, ought not to stand in isolation. It has been said that one of the reasons why the Bible movement, which began after the First World War, soon lost much of its momentum is that it was too academic and not sufficiently linked with the prayer of the Church.[4] Scripture readings, whether in church or in small groups, ought to be understood as the *Capitulum* of one of the

[2] Cf. 'Pour une liturgie catéchuménale' from 'La Messe et sa Catéchèse' in *Lex orandi*, VII, Paris, 1947, pp. 294–8; cf. *ibid.*, pp. 301 ff.; G. Delcuve, *La question du catéchisme en France*, Brussels, 1957, p. 45.

[3] *Directoire pour la pastorale de la Messe*, Paris, 1956, p. 75, n. 256.

[4] T. Schnitzler, 'Das Wort Gottes in der Andacht' in *Anima*, x, 1955, pp. 323–31. Reprinted in *Im Dienste des Wortes*, pp. 81–9 – see note 5.

Hours of prayer, restored to its full significance. At all events it should be concluded with prayer. It should form the core of what we now like to call a liturgy of the Word.

Congregations which have already had considerable experience in this field have made far-reaching suggestions concerning more exact construction and practical execution.[5] We need not go into this topic any further at this point. The important thing to realize is that the word of God deserves a more honoured place in our devotions than it has normally been given. The emphasis in our devotions has usually been placed upon the exposition of the Blessed Sacrament and sacramental Benediction, so that we speak simply of 'Benediction.' In the early Church, and in the liturgical tradition deriving from it, the emphasis was placed clearly upon the liturgy of the Word. When in the Christian assembly the Church reads out the word of Holy Scripture, the redemption which God has planned for us is offered to us afresh: it becomes present. It is neither accidental nor fortuitous that when the Gospel has been read at Mass we greet the Lord as though present: *Gloria tibi, Domine*! This implies no derogation of sacramental Benediction at evening devotions. Without doubt the presence of our Lord in the Blessed Sacrament is closer than in the word: faith is more deeply demanded, and given. On the other hand, it is obvious that the desire for ever fresh forms of Benediction and of receiving a blessing have led to aberrations – not just in the declining Middle Ages. The word of God, being a less close presence, demands a more docile ear. Perhaps it is at this very point that the principle – so much a concern of our separated brethren –

---

[5] Cf. H. Schürmann, 'Die Heilige Schrift im Gemeindeleben' in *Im Dienste des Wortes,* Leipzig, 1959, pp. 54–80. As well as advocating the restoration of the *Capitulum* in the prayer Office, Schürmann advocates 'Bible meetings' where the Scriptures form the central point and are studied meditatively, whether by the congregation or by a smaller group (cf. *can.* 398, C.I.C.).

applies: the Church of the sacrament must be also the Church of the word.

So that the seed of God's word may sink more deeply into the earth, hearing must have a place for meditation. This place can be silence. In the Roman liturgy it is normally the chant, usually a responsory. The responsory is the conclusion – somewhat stultified – of the responsorial psalm-chant, in which a solo singer took up the continued text of the psalm or hymn, the congregation repeating the same verse as a refrain, as we now do in the litanies. It is clear that such refrain-verses, when well chosen, provide an excellent means of inculcating a thought in minds and hearts. The great pastor, St Augustine, may be taken as the classic evidence of the value of such a style of singing.[6] Although neither responsorial singing nor psalmody in general need be the predominant style of singing, the subject deserves a brief consideration.

It is a striking fact that the psalms, which for centuries had dominated the Church's prayer, about the end of the first millennium almost entirely fell out of use, except in the strongly traditional sphere of the liturgy. In Alcuin's time people very largely lived their spiritual life upon the psalms.[7] The basic prayers of the New Testament are, however, more intelligible, and men now began to turn to these. On the other hand something was lost when the psalms almost disappeared from the prayer life of the people, and today something is being gained by their partial re-introduction. As we have said, only certain psalms are suitable, and these we must learn, from the early Church, to interpret in a New Testament sense.[8] The Psalter collects prove that the early Church did not use the psalms as

[6] W. Roetzer, *Des heiligen Augustinus Schriften als liturgiegeschichtliche Quelle,* Munich, 1930, pp. 101 ff.

[7] H. B. Meyer, *Alkuin*, p. 437.

[8] B. Fischer, *Die Psalmenfrömmigkeit der Märtyrerkirche,* Freiburg, 1949.

F

amorphous material, the content of which scarcely interested them. Each psalm was followed by a prayer which expressed the meaning which they thought should be imputed to the psalm. In this way several psalms were strung together, each followed by its own collect.[9] The movement to restore psalm-singing has been specially energetic in France. In Germany it has not moved so swiftly, on account, no doubt, of the wealth of hymns with which tradition had endowed Germany more than other countries. As was only to be expected, these hymns took for their themes the substance of the devotions which have arisen in recent centuries, rather than the themes of the psalms and of the mighty liturgical hymnody of the Church. In many churches, as recently as fifty years ago, the repertoire of hymns was composed mainly of hymns to Mary and hymns in honour of the Sacred Heart. Sometimes these formed the entire repertoire. Meanwhile, however, old treasures have been dug up; and the spirit of religious renewal has added the new to the old. Not least important, many gems of genuine piety have been borrowed from the wealth of hymns enjoyed by our Protestant brethren.[10]

In some way or other the prayer of the assembled congregation must effect a natural transition to the prayer of the priest. This can be accomplished by means of a brief silence – in line with ancient tradition.[11] The Roman and Coptic liturgies have always known the *Flectamus genua*,

---

[9] So, for example, in the old Mozarabic morning Office. Cf. Jungmann, *Pastoral Liturgy*, p. 141; pp. 149 f. On the Christological tone of the Psalter collects cf. F. Vandenbroucke in *Sacris erudiri*, v, 1953, pp. 5–26. A modern advocate of the revival of the psalms with the Psalter collects is D. Rimaud, S.J., in *Maison-Dieu*, LI, 1957, pp. 99–115, esp. 110 ff.

[10] This borrowing of Protestant hymns is not peculiar to our own age. In 1659 the Jesuits published a hymnbook in Vienna, and another like it in 1666 in Trier. Almost two thirds of the hymns were from Protestant sources – B. Fischer, 'Gesangbücher im Trierer Raum' in *Trierer theologische Zeitschrift*, LXV, 1956, p. 46.

[11] According to John Cassian, *De inst. coenob.* II, 7 (*P. L.* XVII, 23 f.), the Egyptian monks used to spend a short time in silent prayer after each psalm, and then the priest said the collect.

the invitation to prayers of petition, said kneeling where possible. In a religiously well-educated congregation, when meditative response to God's word has been made in silence, this silence can clearly provide a transition to the prayer which forms the conclusion of the act of worship.

On other occasions the *Preces* of the Office will occur at this place. The *Preces* have a long history in the public worship of the Church. In the nature of the case they include also the Prayer of the Faithful, the *oratio communis*, which from time immemorial came at the conclusion of the Fore-mass. Responding to the deacon or priest, the congregation pray for all the needs of Christians in the world and in the Church. A welcome revival of this kind of prayer has been achieved by the liturgical movement. The meaning and importance of such prayer has been explained[12] and forms composed which have received approval in different places by ecclesiastical authority, and have been tried and tested in the public worship of congregations.[13] Discussion on the most suitable structure of such prayer,[14] and accumulated

[12] Cf. chiefly J. Gülden, 'Das allgemeine Kirchengebet in der Sicht der Seelsorge' in *Die Messe in der Glaubensverkündigung*, 2nd ed., Freiburg, 1953, pp. 337–53. The importance of this matter was first stressed by J. Wagner: cf. Gülden, p. 337, note 2. It has been historically examined by Jungmann in *The Mass of the Roman Rite*. The tradition of the "prières du prône," alive in France, provided stimulus to the examination of this precious heritage. Cf. P. M. Gy, 'Signification pastorale des prières du prône' in *Maison-Dieu*, xxx, 1952, pp. 125–36.

[13] With the vernacular low Mass we now have the Prayer of the Faithful back again in normal use. A series of officially approved diocesan prayerbooks provide a more or less rich supply of intercessions. Cf. Meissen, *Laudate,* 1953; Münster, *Laudate,* 1955, and the manual *Gottesdienst,* 1955, 1958; Trier, *Gesang- und Gebetbuch,* 1955. This style of prayer had also been accepted in the *Collectio rituum pro omnibus Germaniae diocesibus* (1950) for the rite of anointing the sick and of burial.

[14] In addition to Gülden's discussion we must draw attention to that of E. Lengeling in 'Fürbitten' in *Lexikon für Theologie und Kirche*, iv, 1960, pp. 461 f., and in the manual, *Gottesdienst,* Münster, 1955, pp. 522–7. Cf. also the many texts provided for the most varied occasions, *ibid.*, pp. 527–604. Cf. also the historically supported proposals for the revision of the Breviary by B. Fischer, 'Litania ad Laudes et Vesperas' in *Liturgisches Jahrbuch*, i, 1957, pp. 55–74. It is obvious that the revival of the *Preces*, in so far as they are still provided for common prayer within the Office, must go hand in hand with the revival of intercession in congregational public worship.

experience, will have to show the form in which intercessions can become a fixed element in the Church's prayer. The chief thing under consideration will be the form that lives on in the Eastern liturgies as the *Ectene* and in the Western liturgies as the litany. This is the form of the final and oldest section of the Litany of the Saints. The precentor announces the intentions: 'Be pleased to direct and guard thy holy Church,' and the congregation respond: 'Hear us, we beseech thee.' This verbal arrangement has the advantage of making orderly speech easy, for the faithful know at once when they have to answer. Obviously other methods of response are possible: the venerable and ancient *Kyrie eleison* or 'Lord have mercy' or 'Amen.'

It is in line with ancient tradition to address prayer in this preparatory section to Christ the Lord. This need not be a binding rule. At this preparatory stage it also makes sense to invoke the saints as we find this done in the Litany of the Saints. The true accent, however, will be upon the intercessions. The intentions named there will in part be unchangeable, repeated on every occasion, and in part variable, suited to the occasion, the circumstances, the feast-day. They should not be dragged out into an exhausting series. The Trier hymnbook of 1955 has wisely determined that the number be kept to four petitions, preceded by a triple appeal to Christ (with a relative predication and a 'Have mercy on us!').[15] In other cases, like the burial rite of the German *Collectio rituum* of 1950, an invitation to prayer comes first, followed by mention of the person being prayed for, and then the 'have mercy' of the congregation; the separate petitions come last. The monthly prayer-intentions of the Holy Father, which of all things are suitable subjects for the common prayer of Christians, might be put into such a form as this, and find a place, concisely arranged, in such

[15] *Gesang- und Gebetbuch*, Trier, 1955, pp. 517–22.

collections. The varying needs of diocese and parish, too, ought to be presented to God in this way, thus making the people aware that these are their own needs. In the Latin tradition, the conclusion is supplied by the *oration*.[16] This is not a rule, prescribing that we should copy only the liturgy, but a requirement arising from the nature of the Church's prayer. Religion is a relationship with God, and prayer, where it fully comes into its own, is, in the final analysis, conversation with God, our Creator and Father.

It is not in harmony, therefore, with the objective order of things if, at May-devotions, the Marian theme is so rigidly followed that even the concluding prayer is addressed to the Mother of God. It is most fitting if, following ancient tradition, the Lord's Prayer is used in place of the *oration*. The ancient concluding doxology, too, might fittingly be added in this place: 'For thine is the kingdom . . .' This doxology had already become joined to the Our Father in the second century, perhaps to allow the congregation to join in at this point.[17] Another method would be to have the Lord's Prayer recited solemnly, section by section, the congregation responding 'Amen' each time. We find this style worked out in the Mozarabic tradition.[18] Or again, a suitable *embolismus* might be attached to the Our Father, as is done in the Mass, and in the above-mentioned German Ritual of 1950.

For centuries now it has been traditional to close evening devotions with Benediction of the Blessed Sacrament. Thus, evening devotions have come to be called simply 'Benediction'. Pius XII took this Benediction under his special protection as being in accord with the practice of the

---

[16] The doxology which J. Gülden puts in place of these corresponds to Eastern usage.

[17] This practice is advocated by H. Schürmann, *Das Gebet des Herrn*, Freiburg, 1958, p. 140.

[18] Cf. *P. L.* LXXXV, 559.

Church.[19] Clearly this does not mean that the Blessed Sacrament must be exposed throughout the entire devotion. It can form the conclusion after the fashion of a sublime commemoration: the Church's most precious treasure is taken out and honoured in hymns and prayers, and with it a blessing is imparted, as is the custom prescribed by the Church in many places.[20]

[19] Cf. *Mediator Dei: A.A.S.*, 1947, pp. 569–71. Tr. *Christian Worship* (C.T.S. Do 270), p. 55, sec. 143.

[20] Cf. E. Lengeling in the manual *Gottesdienst,* 1955, p. 111, n. 115. In several German dioceses synodal decrees have prescribed or recommended new diocesan prayerbooks or regulations, and that at devotions (of saints, of our Lady, the Rosary, the Way of the Cross) exposition should not occur until the blessing, or may be omitted. Cf. *ibid.,* 'Aussetzung des Allerheiligsten' in *Unser Gottesdienst*, Freiburg, 1960, pp. 178–90; p. 187.

XVI

Religion and the World

IN THIS book so far we have discussed exclusively the inner world of religion, its symptoms of decline, possibilities of reconstruction, its structural laws, and ideal patterns. In this way have we not, perhaps, lost touch with solid reality? Are we not hovering, if not in a world of unreality, at least in regions that bear no relation to the tangible world of daily experience, to the real world that is to be redeemed, that is to be called back to God?

The danger is that we shall build a religion without a world; and then we shall be surprised to find that we are left with a world without religion.[1] If we do that, then we have falsified religion.

Most certainly some are called to the vocation of the 'spiritual man', to overleap the earthly world, to anticipate the eschatological community of God, in the contemplative life which from time immemorial has remained as a sign raised up within the Church, a kind of lighthouse to point men the way through life to their final destination. But the great mass of men are not called to this life. Religion, however, is meant for them too; theirs is the kingdom of God, the Church, and in the Church, worship, the liturgy.

The liturgy is the very place where the Church is in danger. The Church is tempted to see the liturgy as a transfigured world, a delightful illusion, into which one flees

---

[1] A. Auer, 'Zur theologischen Grundlegung einer christlichen Laienfrömmigkeit' in *Verkündigung und Glaube* (*Festschrift für F.X. Arnold,* Freiburg, 1959), pp. 307-26, esp. 309.

on Sunday to get away for a moment or two from the oppression and vexation of everyday life. We are tempted to become enthusiasts for the liturgy, for sacred music, Latin prayers, for archaic forms a thousand years old, and never to think of throwing a bridge across to the rough everyday world of today. The liturgy itself may be partly to blame. People have even reproached the liturgical movement, that is trying to make the liturgy intelligible and accessible to men, with being 'restorationist', because it works with material that remains intrinsically foreign and incomprehensible.[2] Clearly for years it will remain one of the tasks of the liturgical revival progressively to overcome this strangeness and incomprehensibility, without thereby losing touch with tradition. Liturgy, as well as religion, would be misunderstood were it to become isolated from life. Religion and liturgy have no intention of being self-sufficient institutions and activities, but a call and a testimony that our whole life belongs to God. Our morning or Sunday eucharistic sacrifice especially desires to do nothing other than make sure and fast the link that binds our life to God.

The concentrating of the substance of faith, the clarification of its basic features, the stress upon the good news, which we have made an effort to achieve, all have one purpose: to ensure that the call be more surely heard and that the demand which it makes upon the whole breadth of life be really understood. In times of oppression when so much becomes destroyed, we strengthen the walls of our citadels wherein we gather up all our strength, in preparation for a fresh attack upon life. The Christian faith does not want to be a mere piece of information which we hold on to in the obedience of faith, but a new light shining upon our existence, the knowledge that God has not forgotten us, but is drawing us to himself in amazing, condescending love. We

[2] Ida F. Görres in *Wort und Wahrheit*, xiii, 1958, p. 663.

can scarcely imagine the impression that the Christian message made upon enquiring men in the early days, and what a
revolution it effected in their thought. Justin, philosopher and
martyr, is able to say: '. . . we, who loved nothing like our
possessions, now produce all we have in common, and
spread our whole stock before our indigent brethren;
we who were pointed at with mutual hatred and destruction,
and would not so much as warm ourselves at the same fire
with those of a different tribe upon account of different
institutions, now since the coming of Christ cohabit and
diet together, and pray for our enemies; and all our returns
for evil are but the gentlest persuasions to convert those
who unjustly hate us, that they may be filled with the same
comfortable hopes of attaining the like happiness with
ourselves . . .'[3]

Because the Christian message is a message of God's
magnanimous love, because it is good news, because it
unlocks for us the highest good, therefore wherever it is
properly understood and truly accepted it is bound to
become a tremendous impulse, the power of which takes
hold of the whole of life, and can be felt in every last
expression of that life.[4] At the same time this means that
it goes beyond the spiritual poverty and meanness of
legalistic morality[5] which is content at all times scantily to
fulfil the minimal requirements, comforting itself with the
principle: *Finis legis non cadit sub lege*. It means that there is
an autonomous Christian judgement at work concerning the
things of this world, especially where we are concerned with

---

[3] Justin, *Apology* I, c. 14., in Ancient and Modern Library of Theological Literature, London, 1889, p. 19.

[4] To this corresponds the presentation of the whole of Christian doctrine under
two headings – to some extent as a drama between God and man: the work of
divine grace in Christ (doctrine of faith), and man's response in gratitude and love
(doctrine of morals). Cf. J. Hofinger, *The Art of Teaching Christian Dogma*, 2nd ed.,
Notre Dame, Indiana, 1962.

[5] Cf. B. Häring, *Das Gesetz Christi*, I, 6th ed., Freiburg, 1961, pp. 84 f.; p. 240 ff.

progress, culture, art, welfare, and joy in living. It means
that there is a capacity for Christian discrimination.[6] It
means the readiness to get right down to the true meaning
of things, as they are in the plan of God's creation, thus
contributing towards the perfecting of the cosmos and the
glory of the Creator.[7] In recent decades theology has been
applying itself in a welcome way to these tasks. A 'theology
of secular realities' has emerged.[8] We have become more
clearly aware that God speaks to us through creation, and
reveals his will to us in the possibilities set down in the
created order; that therefore we do not glorify God best
by bringing an external 'good intention' to our use of earthly
things, but by coming to terms with these things, by adopt-
ing the right attitude to them and using them in accordance
with their divinely decreed nature. These demands that
are laid down in creation are not cancelled by Christian
revelation, but, on the contrary, by the Incarnation of the
Logos, who entered this world and became obedient to
its laws to the very end, the intrinsic value of worldly
reality has been well and truly underlined. The Incarnation
is the beginning of the new creation. The continuation of the
new creation can proceed, therefore, only upon the foundation of the Incarnation, upon the affirmation of earthly
realities, as these realities are given to us both in the

[6] 'Christian discrimination' was the significant title of a collection of essays
(1935) by Romano Guardini, one of the most important early champions of this
new mentality. The task proposed in this work is far from having been successfully
accomplished, as a review in *Wort und Wahrheit*, VIII, 1953, p. 887, points out.
Liberation from the ghetto, it says, 'has not led to the reformation of secular culture,
but to assimilation to it.'

[7] Living Christianity even in a technical age will never be content with a revived
'consciousness of the ultimate helplessness of Christianity in the secular-social
sphere.' Cf. A. Mirgeler, *Rückblick auf das abendländische Christentum*, Mainz, 1961,
p. 51. Mirgeler alleges that this defeatism is implied by the Antichrist passages of
the Apocalypse.

[8] This is led by G. Thils, *Théologie des réalités terrestres*, Bruges, 1946–9. Cf. the
vigorous point of view of D. Thalhammer, *Zeitschrift für katholische Theologie*, LXXIV,
1952, pp. 83–90.

external world and in the social life of the family, the State, and profession.[9]

The new impulse which the Christian receives from the living message must, therefore, show itself in competent work within this world, in the care with which the workman tends his machinery, in the human devotion the official brings to his duties, in the sacrifice with which the mother looks after her children: in short, in the conscientiousness with which each man fulfils the most material, worldly task.

In our times, if ever, when so much physical work is performed with the help of machinery, man should be able to rise above the drudgery of manual labour and allow the spirit to come into its own. The cultural flowering of the late Middle Ages, which must have had very limited tools to work with, disposed of leisure with a royal magnanimity, spending it not only in a considerable number of religious feast-days, but from time to time enlisted the whole community in the performance of mystery plays, which would elevate men for days on end into a higher world. Drama in classical times, too, had a similar origin. It would be most fitting, then, for us, to whom has fallen an extra share of leisure, to use that time generously in spiritual pursuits, and to help our souls in their ascent to a higher world. All reasonable use of leisure is, in any case, an entering into a spiritually ordered world.

Admittedly, everything depends upon the fundamental decision for the faith being made in calm certainty, and held firm. This is more difficult now than in former days. The reason for this is not simply because the naïve credulity of our forefathers, which saw direct divine intervention in every unusual event, is no longer possible in these days of

[9] Cf. amongst others, A. Auer, *Zur theologischen Grundlegung einer christlichen Laienfrömmigkeit,* pp. 320 ff.

sober natural science. Nor is it because technology has
surrounded our lives with so much man-made machinery
that our vision of God's works has become seriously
obstructed – although we should indeed recognize and
admire God's creative power in these very things, and see
man not as his robot but as his co-planner and co-creative
master of this technical world. It is because for two centuries
science within the Church has become entangled in battles
along the frontiers of faith, which of necessity have repeatedly directed attention towards those very points
where attack is possible, whether in the field of natural
science or of history. The result of these battles has often
been a sharp fixing of frontiers, and certainly this has only
hardened the attitude of faith. As in philosophy the study
of the psychological contingency of our knowledge
signifies all the greater certainty for our true knowledge,
so it is in the theological-religious field. Thus, *Form-
geschichte*, by interpreting many of the texts of Scripture,
which we read so ingenuously, in terms of the formative
tradition that was at work between the event and the scriptural recording of that event, is able to give us a more exact
account of what really is recorded. But it robs us of our
guileless ingenuousness. There are exegetical publications
which seem to consist of nothing but marginal emendations
that can be read only with an effort. Our attention is need-
lessly fixed upon side-issues which do nothing to alter the
account as a whole. In the end the figure of Christ stands
before us unexplained and inexplicable as always: his
incomparable appearance, his self-testimony, his resurrection, and his Church, too, 'the sign amongst the nations,'
remain for ever the same.

The impression is deepened, however, that infallible
faith is a grace that we could never hold on to without a
constantly renewed humble turning to God in prayer, with-

out a permanently preserved openness to God's call. And we are more clearly conscious that revelation is not given in order to provide us with unlimited knowledge of divine things, enabling us to name and define everything in heaven and on earth, but so that we may be content that a way has been shown us through this world's darkness, a way that is adequately illumined by the light of heaven, so that we shall be able to complete our pilgrimage supported by the confidence of Christian hope.

This confidence of Christian hope does not mean that our journey will be without its trials. We have long since accepted the fact that although God the Lord has intervened mightily in the course of the world through the events of salvation-history, yet in the normal course of things he leaves his beloved children at the mercy of the laws of the natural order he has himself established. Not only are his people exposed to accidents, diseases, and natural catastrophes, just like all the children of men, but they must look after themselves, using all the means of human inventiveness, all the arts of medicine, all the methods of prudent insurance and social welfare. Christianity has no desire to alter the external conditions of human life.

Our pilgrimage is surrounded by much darkness; but the greater the darkness, the brighter does the light of heaven shine upon our path, and all the more thankfully do we grasp the hand of him who came from above to lead us, all the more enthusiastically do we apply our strength for the *Ecclesia peregrinans*, so that even here upon earth God will be glorified in Christ and in his Church.

The kingdom of God must already start growing upon this earth. Not for nothing did Christ the Lord compare his kingdom with the sprouting seed, the grain of mustard, and with leaven. The kingdom of God must grow and Christ must rule. But he does not wish to rule through the application of secular power, but, as the Fathers of the Church reiterate: *per fidem credentium*. The fervour of our faith is the power that will once again inspire the dead mass of a God-estranged civilization – if there be but sufficient faith. Faith growing in our hearts, must produce forms which will give it expression and support. Christian customs are of the greatest importance here, but Christian customs can be healthily grown only from living faith. It is of no use trying to keep alive dead forms. New and vigorous forms are already growing around the inner sanctuary. The candle that is lit from the paschal candle at the Easter Vigil is already carrying thoughts of Easter back into the family. Christian art is beginning to bloom once more; our new church architecture is a sign of this. In a violently changing age the Church will prove her eternal youth. Ida Frederike Görres is right: 'The signs are being multiplied that in the deserts of Christendom men are again seeking the ancient wells. They are digging and removing mud. Water-diviners are hearing the captive water rushing underground. Many things suggest that, besides the obvious stream that is careering along at increasing distance from God, another has erupted which is growing, still underground and scarcely perceptible, but steadily and full of promise.'[10]

---

[10] Ida F. Görres, *Der göttliche Bettler und andere Versuche,* Frankfurt, 1959, p. 220.

Index